George Washington, Worthington Chauncey Ford

The Spurious Letters Attributed to Washington

George Washington, Worthington Chauncey Ford
The Spurious Letters Attributed to Washington
ISBN/EAN: 9783337817718
Printed in Europe, USA, Canada, Australia, Japan
Cover: Foto ©Thomas Meinert / pixelio.de

More available books at **www.hansebooks.com**

THE

SPURIOUS LETTERS

ATTRIBUTED TO

WASHINGTON.

—

WITH

A BIBLIOGRAPHICAL NOTE

BY

WORTHINGTON CHAUNCEY FORD.

BROOKLYN, N. Y.:
PRIVATELY PRINTED.
1889,

CONTENTS.

	PAGE
PREFACE	5
BIBLIOGRAPHY	38

THE SPURIOUS LETTERS.

To Lund Washington, June 12, 1776	45
To John Parke Custis, June 18, 1776	59
To the Hon. Lady Washington, June 24, 1776	69
To Mr. Lund Washington, July 16, 1776	80
To Mr. Lund Washington, July 8, 1776	87
To Mr. Lund Washington, July 15, 1776	98
To Mr. Lund Washington, July 22, 1776	112

THE CAREY COLLECTION OF "OFFICIAL LETTERS."

John Carey	123
Jefferson to Carey	125
Carey to Jefferson	125
Carey to Washington	127
Carey to Jefferson	128
Carey to Washington	129
Carey to Washington	135
Jefferson to Carey	136

HOW WASHINGTON BECAME COMMANDER-IN-CHIEF	138
LIFE AND CHARACTER OF GENERAL WASHINGTON, 1778	148
CHARACTER OF WASHINGTON, 1779	154
THE AURORA'S FAREWELL TO WASHINGTON, 1797	157
INDEX	161

PREFACE.

In May or June, 1777, there appeared in London a pamphlet, bearing the imprint of J. Bew, a bookseller in Paternoster Row, purporting to contain certain letters of Washington written in 1776, to his friends and relatives in Virginia. There can be little doubt that the issue was calculated to attain some end. Were the letters genuine, they would be of interest as showing that Washington was playing a part as commander in chief of the American army, leading a cause for which he had little or no sympathy, and under the burden and discouragement of which, even at this early period of the war, he was becoming disheartened, and longing for a full reconciliation with the mother country. A two-fold object could be accomplished, were this the case. It would strengthen the war party in England, give aid to the ministry to push the issue, and endorse the idea that the contest would be speedily terminated by the complete overthrow of the rebellion in the Colonies, and the reëstablishment of the authority of king and Parliament in those dependencies. From this standpoint it would not be very strange if some one connected with the government party had had some agency in publishing, if not in preparing, the letters;

letters; but from another, private pique may have suggested the idea. For on reaching America, the letters might discredit Washington with the American army and the people, and by occasioning suspicions of his integrity, introduce dissensions into the councils of the "rebels."

The compiler of the letters was certainly very shrewd in preparing his preface explaining the manner in which he obtained, or rather was supposed to have obtained, the manuscripts. He modestly called himself the "editor," and paved the way for obtaining the credence of the public as follows:

The public will naturally be inquisitive as to the authenticity of the following letters. For everything else they will speak for themselves: and, for their genuineness, the editor conceives himself concerned to give only such vouchers as he himself has received. By the last pacquet he was favored with a letter from a friend, now serving in a loyal corps under Brigadier-General Delancey, of New York, of which he here subjoins a faithful extract. Pleased with the communication himself (and, as he is not ashamed to add, instructed by it), he could not be easy to withhold it from the public at large: inasmuch as, in his judgment, it exhibits a fairer and fuller view of American politics than the world has seen.

"Among the prisoners at Fort Lee, I espied a mulatto fellow, whom I thought I recollected, and who confirmed my conjectures by gazing very earnestly at me. I asked him if he knew me. At first, he was unwilling to own it; but, when he was about to be carried off, thinking, I suppose, that I might perhaps be of some service to him, he came and told me that he was Billy, and the old servant of General Washington. He had been left there on account of an indisposition

sition which prevented his attending his master. I asked him a great many questions, as you may suppose; but found very little satisfaction in his answers. At last, however, he told me that he had a small portmanteau of his master's; of which, when he found that he must be put into confinement, he intreated my care. It contained only a few stockings and shirts; and I could see nothing worth my care, except an almanack, in which he had kept a journal, or diary, of his proceedings since his first coming to New York: there were also two letters from his lady, one from Mr. Custis, and some pretty long ones from a Mr. Lund Washington, and in the same bundle with them, the first draughts, or foul copies, of answers to them. I read these with avidity; and being highly entertained with them, have shewn them to several of my friends, who all agree with me, that he is a very different character from what they had supposed him. I never knew a man so much to be pitied. If I remember right, you have seen, and have some knowledge of him; but it is impossible you could form so just an estimate as these letters will give you. They contain also, as you will find, a deal of information not to be had anywhere else: I assure myself, therefore, you will thank me for the trouble I have taken in copying them for your perusal."

Fort Lee was taken on November 20th, 1776, the American army leaving so hastily as to lose the "whole of the cannon that were at the fort, except two twelve-pounders, and a great deal of baggage, between two and three hundred tents, about a thousand barrels of flour, and other stores in the quartermaster's department. This loss was inevitable."—*Washington to the President of Congress*, 21 November, 1776. In such a hasty retreat it was very reasonable to suppose that

that some of the sick might have been left behind in the confusion, and so "Billy" was taken.

Washington did have a very trusted "mulatto man" calling himself William Lee, and probably the boy who was purchased of Mary Lee in 1768 for £61.15. The name William, a very common one among slaves, is entered each year among the tithables returned by Washington, and always among the house servants. He was doubtless the successor of Washington's old body servant, John Bishop, said to have been Braddock's servant, and John Alton. Billy or William was so highly appreciated by Washington, that in making his will, he gave him the alternative of "immediate freedom, or, if he should prefer it, (on account of the accidents which have befallen him, and which have rendered him incapable of walking, or of any active employment,) to remain in the situation he now is . . in either case, however, I allow him an annuity of thirty dollars, during his natural life, which shall be independent of the victuals and clothes he has been accustomed to receive, if he chooses the last alternative; but in full with his freedom, if he prefers the first; and this I give him, as a testimony of my sense of his attachment to me, and for his faithful services during the Revolutionary war." So that in the preface at least, the editor apparently takes the public into his confidence, leaves nothing of his knowledge untold, and by a judicious assortment of names and events, weaves a story that might have deceived an intimate friend of Washington, so correct does it appear.

It

It should be remembered that the English public had almost none of the means of checking the statements made in the letters themselves, where the fabricator so often makes gross inaccuracies of statement, impossible combinations of events, and threads together in fantastic array a narrative that will not bear the slightest investigation. For example, it is now known that about the middle of August, 1776, Washington sent to Philadelphia all his papers, lest in the campaign near New York they should fall into the hands of the enemy. Is it likely that he and Billy would be carrying with them in November private letters that were written four or five months previously, and especially when no part of the public papers were returned to him until the end of December? Moreover, the English public had been crammed for some time with rumors and tales that would seem to bear out much that the writer states of the dissatisfaction, amounting almost to disgust, of Washington with his position. It was a common thing to make him a prisoner, or even to kill him in a battle; so also, to vary the tale, he was made to quarrel with Congress, with his generals, and, in a pet, to throw up his commission. The readers of the newspapers of the day were thus in a measure prepared for just such sentiments as these spurious letters contained. Yet there is no evidence that their publication created any stir, or even attracted much attention. I can find no mention of them in any memoir or collection of letters; and were it not for the notices of the pamphlet in the magazines, the very existence of the publication might be doubted.

The *Monthly Review* merely said: "We cannot look upon

upon these letters as genuine ; but we must pronounce them well written : they would do great honor to General Washington, could his claim to them be indisputably established." The *Critical Review* expressed the same doubt of their reliability. "It is difficult to determine their authenticity from any intrinsic evidence. They contain no facts of a private nature, and they discover not only sentiment, but a correctness of composition." And a third magazine the *Town and Country Magazine*, devoted only two lines to them : "These letters are well written, but whether genuine or not we will not pretend to determine." The letter to Mrs. Washington was printed in the *Gentleman's Magazine*, in 1777, as "an intercepted original letter from Gen. Washington to his lady, having every internal mark of authenticity." It also appeared in the *London Chronicle*, 30 December, 1776, and with the head line " For the *London Chronicle*." Instead of being addressed to "The Hon. Lady Washington," as in Bew, both the *Gentleman's Magazine* and the *London Chronicle* say "Mrs. Washington, etc." The publisher, John Bew, died April 12th, 1793, and was then a bookseller in Paternoster Row. He was the Tory publisher, and issued the *Political Magazine*.

It was not long before these letters reached America, where they were reprinted, presumably by the Tories, who hoped by such means to discredit Washington with the army and people. The letter to Mrs. Washington was printed as a broadside, and again as "an intercepted letter from General Washington to his lady in the year 1776." Mr. Hildeburn, in his valuable

"Issues

"Issues of the Press of Pennsylvania," credits the issue of this single folio sheet to Philadelphia; but I am inclined to believe that it was printed in New York. Washington wrote to Richard Henry Lee, February 15th, 1778: "I have seen a letter published in a handbill at New York, and extracts from it republished in a Philadelphia paper, said to be from me to Mrs. Washington, not one word of which did I ever write." Certainly James Rivington would have been as likely as any one to give circulation to such a letter, and he seized upon the others, to publish them in his *Royal Gazette*.

The letter to Lund Washington, and the introduction of the forger, were published in the *Gazette* of February 14th, 1778; in the issue of the 21st may be found the letter to John Parke Custis, with an explanatory note that "Mr. Custis is the son of Mr. Washington's lady, by a former husband;" in the issue of the 28th, no less than three to Lund Washington were printed, but by some error the dates became altered from the Bew edition. What is dated the 16th July, 1776, in Bew, became the 8th in Rivington, and the 8th of Bew, became the 16th in Rivington. On March 7th, 1778, the letter to Lund Washington of July 22d, 1776, was published, closing the series, as that to Mrs. Washington does not seem to have appeared in the columns of the *Gazette*.

It was three weeks before the letters reached Philadelphia to be copied from the *Royal New York Gazette* (for in those days editors were quite scrupulous in giving credit to those papers from which they borrowed, although

although little else was done than to borrow from outside sources) into the *Royal Pennsylvania Gazette*, published by James Robertson, who had formerly, in association with the poet John Trumbull, published the *Norwich Packet*, at Norwich, Connecticut. The introduction to the letters, and that to Lund of 12 June, 1776, was printed in the *Royal Pennsylvania Gazette* of Friday, 6 March, 1778. The issue of March 17th contained the letter to Custis, and the three letters to Lund, dated respectively, 8th, 16th and 15th of July. On March 14th, the *Philadelphia Ledger*, a paper long suspected of being in the British influence, whose publisher, James Humphreys, Jr., had been driven from the place in November, 1776, to return with the British occupation, began the series in the usual way, with the introduction and the letter to Lund of June 12th; on the 21st, the letter to Custis, and two to Lund—July 8th and July 16th—appeared; and on March 25th, the letter of July 15th to Lund. Not until the 7th of April does the letter to Mrs. Washington seem to have been made public, when Robertson reproduced it in the columns of his *Gazette*.* It is hardly likely, therefore, that the handbill could have originated in Philadelphia, and have circulated for so long a period as to have given rise to Washington's letter of February 15th, just quoted.

Almost immediately, and from Rivington's type, the columns being merely cut up into pages, the entire number were collected in a little pamphlet. A fac

---

* I owe these facts concerning the dates of the Philadelphia issues to my brother, Paul Leicester Ford.

simile

simile of the title page is given on the opposite page. That it was Rivington's issue is shown by the error of dates which remained uncorrected in the pamphlet, by the style of type, and by the announcement of its issue in the *Gazette* of March 14, 1778,—"*This day are published, Price 2s.* LETTERS from General Washington to several of his friends in the year 1776," etc. In a few weeks, the advertisement was changed so as to read "LETTERS from MR. WASHINGTON to his wife, his Son-in-law, and Mr. Lund Washington; in which," etc. And to swell the pamphlet the letter of Parson Duché to Washington, which had been printed in the *Royal Gazette* on the 29th of November, 1777, and Col. Parke's reply, were added, together with the letter to Mrs. Washington.

Mr. Hildeburn credits this pamphlet to Philadelphia, but we can again refer to Washington as authority that it was from New York that at least one, and perhaps the only publication emanated. In 1788, while Mathew Carey was publishing the *American Museum*, he obtained an extract of a letter purporting to have been written by the President, and which he proposed to reprint in the columns of his magazine. Before doing so, he submitted the matter to Washington, and called out the following reply:

MOUNT VERNON, 27 October 1788.

SIR: In reply to yours of the 20th of this month, I have to observe, that the fragment of the letter in question, supposed to be written by me, is spurious, and that there was a pamphlet containing a great many letters of the same description published in New York at the same time. It should farther be observed, that

that this publication was made soon after several of my
letters were really intercepted with the mail, and that
the pretended copies of them not only blended many
truths with many falsehoods, but were evidently written
by some person exceedingly well acquainted with
my domestic and general concerns. Advantage was
adroitly taken of this knowledge to give the greater
appearance of probability to the fiction.

From these circumstances you will perceive, sir, how
prudently you have acted in making an application to
me previous to your meditated republication. Otherwise I might have found myself under the necessity of
denying that they were genuine, from an apprehension
that being thus preserved in a manner under my eye
and with my acquiescence, they must have assumed the
seal of veracity in the estimation of posterity. For,
whatever credit some of these letters might be thought
to have done to my literary or political talents, I certainly cannot choose to avail myself of the imposition.

With due regard, I am, etc.

It was either this pamphlet, or a copy of the English
issue, that reached the hands of Richard Henry Lee.
"The arts of the enemies of America are endless, but
all wicked as they are various. Among other tricks
they have forged a pamphlet of letters, entitled 'Letters
from General Washington to several of his friends in
1776.' The design of the forger is evident, and no
doubt it gained him a good beefsteak from his masters.
I would send you this pamphlet, if it were not too
bulky for the post, as it might serve to amuse your
leisure hours during the inaction of winter."* This
was apparently the first intimation that Washington
received of such letters being in currency, and men-

---

* Quoted in Sparks, *Writings of Washington*, v. 237.

tioning

tioning the broadside issue of the supposed missive to Mrs. Washington, he replied: "Those contained in the pamphlet you speak of are, I presume, equally genuine, and perhaps written by the same author. I should be glad, however, to see and examine the texture of them, if a favorable opportunity to send them should present."* It was not until May that Lee found such an opportunity, and he added, "'Tis among the pitiful arts of our enemies to endeavor at sowing dissentions among the friends of liberty and their country. With me, such tricks can never avail."† A cursory examination enabled Washington to recognize the falsity of the letters, and at the same time the skill with which they had been pieced together.

"These letters are written with a great deal of art. The intermixture of so many family circumstances (which, by the by, want foundation in truth) gives an air of plausibility, which renders the villainy greater; as the whole is a contrivance to answer the most diabolical purposes. Who the author of them is, I know not. From information, or acquaintance, he must have had some knowledge of the component parts of my family; but he has most egregiously mistaken facts in several instances. The design of his labors is as clear as the sun in its meridian brightness." ‡ To Landon Carter—the same who is mentioned in one of the forged letters—he wrote:

I am sorry it is not in my power to furnish you with

---
* *Washington to Lee*, 15 February, 1778.
† *Lee to Washington*, 6 May, 1778.
‡ *Washington to Lee*, 25 May, 1778.

the

the letter required, which, with many others, was written to show, that I was an enemy to independence, and with a view to create distrust and jealousy. I never had but one of them, and that I sent to Mrs. Washington, to let her see what obliging folks there are in the world. As a sample of it, I inclose to you another letter, written for me to Mr. Custis, of the same tenor, which I happen to have by me. It is no easy matter to decide, whether the villainy or artifice of these letters is greatest. They were written by a person who had some knowledge or information of the component parts of my family, and yet they are so deficient in circumstances and facts, as to run into egregious misrepresentations of both.*

But the matter did not rest here, for again were the letters to be laid before the public as historical material. A Mr. John Carey had obtained Washington's sanction for an English editon of his letters to the Continental Congress during the Revolution, and in 1795 two volumes were published in London, as the beginning of a collection of "American State Papers, being a collection of original and authentic Documents relative to the War between the United States and Great Britain.

---

* Letter of 30th May, 1778.

Landon Carter had written : "My dear General can oblige much with a copy of the famous printed letter that was forg'd for him to his lady in Philadelphia, published in one of the papers, June 24, 1776. I have never seen or heard of it, till y^r quondam ade de camp informed me of it this March. A curious performance I understand it to be ; and so replete with your domestic occurences, that it deservedly lodges a suspicion of its inventor somewhere near to you. Your local country are unanimously devoted to y^r protection. And let Gates, Mifflin, and the Hy—te Conway, raise what disturbances they can think of, you have an asilum here in every honest breast. For my part I do so abominate ingratitude, to so much virtue as yours in particular, that had not a grand infirmity prevented it, I should long ago have been in Congress to have died inch by inch for you."—*MS. letter.*

Published

Published by special permission."* Although the work was never completed, for the volumes contained the correspondence only to the end of 1778, it was republished in America in the same year (1795). A Boston edition bears this date on its title page,† and a second edition was printed in 1796. In the latter year a New York issue was apparently made, but it was really published by September, 1795. The New York *Daily Advertiser* of September 10, 1795, announced the two volumes as published on that day, but without the name of the printer or publisher. The announcement continued:

"Respecting the source from which the following letters have been drawn, and the grounds on which the reader expects to rest his belief of their authenticity, it may be sufficient to inform him, that permission was obtained from the proper authority to transcribe, from the original papers preserved in the Secretary of State's Office, in Philadelphia, these and sundry other documents, relating to the contest between Great Britain and the United States.

"The reasoning, philosophic reader will, from a perusal of these letters, be able to explore the secret springs of action during the contest, to trace events to their remote and latent causes, and to discover and examine the subordinate and collateral circumstances (oft

---

* I give in an appendix some of Carey's letters concerning this collection.

† "A clear refutation of the calumny against the President of the United States, on the subject of Independence, may be seen in the volumes of Official Letters to Congress, just now published." *Columbia Centinel*, Boston, 2 September, 1795.

trifling

trifling in appearance, and generally overlooked by the vulgar eye) which in the struggle of contending nations give a preponderancy to the one or the other scale. They contain a history of the leading events of the war, and the heroism, love of country and many amiable virtues which are conspicuous in almost every letter, would, were it possible, tend to endear the name and memory of the author, to his grateful country, and the world of mankind."

A few days later the same sheet announced that the volume was to be sold by "J. Rivington, at No. 156, in Pearl street," and Rivington's advertisement contained the paragraphs just quoted. The *Minerva* stated that these letters, "highly interesting and entertaining," could be had at its office, for 20s., the English edition selling for four dollars. The editor of that newspaper, Noah Webster, wrote of these volumes on the 16th :

"The men who abuse our Chief Magistrate or attempt to detach from his administration the confidence of the American public, ought to read his letters to Congress, now published in two volumes, and of which we have a few copies at the office of this paper.

"No man who reviews his arduous struggles, during the late war, with difficulties almost insurmountable; raw troops, without discipline, clothing, arms, powder or other military apparatus; a discontented, fickle militia, without order or subordination; an empty military chest; state jealousies, and innumerable tories—I say no man, who reads his letters in which
all

all these difficulties are most feelingly described, can readily withdraw his attachment from this firm, unshaken patriot, or willingly abandon himself to a suspicion of his integrity."

The publication was made at a very critical period of our history, as the whole country was in a ferment over the Jay treaty. This document had been divulged by the treachery of a Senator—Mason—and had stirred the political factions of the nation as they had never been stirred before. Washington had signed the treaty, and the French party denounced him as an enemy to the country, a traitor to liberty, a political hypocrite—in fact, the embodiment of all that was mischievous, dangerous and wicked. The opposition opened upon him the flood-gates of abuse and libel, in a manner that astonished and shocked many of Washington's opponents in that day, in a manner that would put to shame the most rabid partisan penny-a-liner of the present day. No terms of opprobrium were so violent, and no attempt to defame and discredit his character was so mean, as not to be useful to the purposes of these writers. The issue of Washington's war correspondence only seemed to inspire the pens of these libellers, and to increase their scandalous boldness of attack and methods. One may be cited as an example:

"Suffer me to observe once for all, that in the analysis of your political character, I shall be constrained to show myself more the enemy of your heart than of your head. I promise not to wound your self-love, by the ambiguous apology for your conduct which has so often flowed from the lips of those who call themselves your

your friends. *They* could vouch for your political *honesty;* on the score of *wisdom*, they have generally been silent. In the character of a *general*, you possessed the undisputed palm of eminence; in that of a politician, your modesty forebore laying claim to the deep views of a statesman, or the crafty wiles of a courtier! Hence, whatever deviations from the constitutional orbit may have marked your political course, have arisen from the deficiency of your knowledge, or from misdirection of your mind by the erroneous information of others!"*

Among the charges brought against Washington at this time was one that asserted he had been too great a friend of English interests during his presidency, and even during the Revolution. And in proof of the latter assertion the spurious letters of 1776 would be of service. On the very day after the New York issue of his official letters was announced, the *Daily Advertiser* published an "extract of a letter (published as authentic) from the President of the United States, to Mr. Lund Washington, written in 1776." The extract was a few sentences from the letter of June 12th, 1776 and read as follows:

"Do not mistake me—I thank my God, I have never yet known what it was to fear for any personal danger that might befal me! I am not afraid to die, why should I? I am afraid only to die with infamy and disgrace. And, if I am afraid so to die, need I tell

---

* *Valerius*, in the Aurora. I have reprinted in the appendix the famous, or rather infamous, words printed by that paper on Washington's retirement.

that

that I am ten thousand times more afraid to live like Lucifer, a fallen angel. No, Lund, that were too much; betide what will, I cannot, I will not survive either my misfortunes or my disgraces. Heaven knows how truly I love my country!"

This was published September 11, 1795, and two months later (9 December, 1795), the *Daily Advertiser* contained a notice that "General Washington's letters to several of his friends in 1776," had just been received by Fellows and Adams, on Water street, price two shillings. This was presumably copies of the pamphlet issued from the "Federal Press" of Philadelphia, containing the seven spurious letters, and a preface which read as follows:

"The following letters are, at this time, republished from a Boston edition, now out of print, as furnishing an interesting appendix to the official letters of GENERAL WASHINGTON, which have lately made their appearance."

I fear the mention of a Boston edition was put in as a blind, as I am unable to trace any such issue.

A few months after the publication of the New York edition of the genuine "official letters," the spurious letters were reprinted in that city with an appendix containing a number of other letters and documents, making a very respectable volume of about three hundred pages. The intent of this republication was explained with no little art in the preface, although it will be noted that not one word respecting their authenticity is given.

Since

Since the publication of the two volumes of General Washington's *Original Letters to the Congress*, the Editor has been repeatedly applied to for the General's *Domestic and Confidential Epistles*, first published soon after the beginning of the American war. These Epistles are here offered to the public,* together with a copious appendix, containing a number of *Official Letters and Papers*, not to be found in the General's *Original Letters*, lately published.

The world is, without doubt, greatly indebted to the industrious compiler of the two volumes of *Original Letters*, above noticed, but the collection must certainly be looked upon as in a mutilated state, so long as it remains unaccompanied with the Epistles, etc., which are now respectfully submitted to the patronage of the public, and which form a supplement absolutely necessary to render the work complete.

That this collection of *Domestic and Confidential Epistles* will be regarded as a valuable acquisition by a very great majority of the citizens of the United States, is presumable from the prevailing taste of all well-informed people. Men not precluded by ignorance from every degree of literary curiosity, will always feel a solicitude to become acquainted with whatever may serve to throw light on the characters of illustrious personages. History represents them acting on the stage of the world, courting the applause of mankind; to see them in their real character, we must follow them behind the scenes, among their private connections and domestic concerns.

Nor is this kind of inquisitiveness to be ascribed to an ill-natured desire of discovering the foibles of those who tower above us in talents of virtue, with an intention of levelling them to our own standard; it has a much more amiable source; which is, no other than a na-

---

* The full titles are given in the Bibliographical note at the end of this introduction.

tural

tural propensity in the generality of mankind to find something to commend in even the most insignificant actions of those they admire. The inconceivable pains that have been taken to come at the domestic anecdotes of Shakespeare, could certainly have no motive but the laudable one of obtaining some endearing memorial of a man, whose fame will never die but with the language in which he wrote.

If, then, this propensity is praiseworthy when the subject of enquiry relates to persons of literary fame, it must be so in a ten-fold degree when it relates to a man so eminently exalted as he to whom these Epistles are attributed ; for, however, great may be the services of the former, however their labors may have added to our pleasures, softened our manners, enlarged our understandings, and improved our hearts, yet are they of an order inferior to those which rescue an Empire from ruin, give happiness to millions, and enable them to transmit it to their children's children. Even abstracted from all considerations relating to self, where is the man whose every sentiment so well deserves to be remembered ? In whom was there ever seen such an assemblage of virtues? To him belongs the rare felicity of uniting zeal with moderation, firmness with prudence, and courage with circumspection. We may challenge the world to produce a hero who, like him, has attained to the highest pinnacle of honor, without staining his career with a single crime.

Not to know how to prize the good they possess, is but too often the misfortune of mankind ; we must not, therefore, be surprised, if some Americans should be found totally indifferent as to such anecdotes as do honor to our illustrious chief magistrate, and others who seek for such only as may tend to produce a contrary effect ; but we may rest assured that the time will come, when even those who are now vainly endeavoring to cast a shade over his virtues and his services,
will

will think themselves happy in possessing the slightest testimony of their veneration for his memory.

The delicate irony that prompted the insertion of such a preface in a book where all the truth was relegated to the appendix, and even there in a garbled shape, and where old untruths were resurrected to serve as a "campaign document" to the discredit of the alleged writer, seems to have struck Washington, and induced him to take steps to repudiate once for all any connection with these letters. As Rivington was the seller of this book, and as he had been instrumental in giving the letters currency in 1778, Washington naturally thought of applying to him for information respecting the real writer. Unwilling to have any direct communication with the former Loyal printer, Washington wrote to Colonel Benjamin Walker, one of his former aids, who held the office of naval officer of New York in Washington's administration. His letter was as follows:

PHILADELPHIA, 12 January, 1797.

DEAR WALKER: * * * If you read the *Aurora* of this city, or those gazettes which are under the same influence, you cannot but have perceived with what malignant industry and perservering falsehoods I am assailed, in order to weaken if not to destroy the confidence of the public.

Amongst other attempts to effect this purpose, spurious letters, known at the time of their first publication (I believe in the year 1777) to be forgeries, to answer a similar purpose in the revolution, are (or extracts from them) brought forward with the highest emblazoning of which they are susceptible, with a view to attach principles to me which every action of my life

has

has given the lie to. But that is no stumbling-block with the editors of these papers and their supporters. And now, perceiving a disinclination on my part, and perhaps knowing that I had determined not to take notice of such attacks, they are pressing this matter upon the public mind with more earnestness than usual, urging that my silence is a proof of their genuineness.

Although I never wrote, nor ever saw one of these letters until they issued from New York in print, yet the author of them must have been tolerably well acquainted in or with some person of my family, to have given the names and some circumstances, which are grouped in the mass of erroneous details. But, of all the mistakes which have been committed in this business, none is more palpable, or susceptible of detection, than the manner in which it is said they were obtained, by the capture of my mulatto Billy, with a portmanteau. All the army under my immediate command could contradict this, and I believe most of them know, that no attendant of mine, nor a particle of my baggage, ever fell into the hands of the enemy during the whole course of the war.

It would be a singular satisfaction to me to learn who was the author of the letters, and from what source they originated. No person in this country can, I conceive, give this information but Mr. Rivington. If, therefore, you are upon terms of familiarity with that gentleman, and see no impropriety in hinting this desire to him, by doing it you would oblige me. He may comply to what extent his own judgment shall dictate; and I pledge my honor, that nothing to his disadvantage, or the disadvantage of any of the actors of that time, shall result from it.

So far as the record shows, Washington's curiosity was not satisfied; and the opposition still harping upon these

these "campaign stories,"—although Adams was about to step into the President's chair—he recorded among the last of his official acts, the falsity of these letters:

"I suffered every attack, that was made upon my executive conduct (the one first mentioned among the rest), to pass unnoticed while I remained in public office, well knowing, that, if the general tenor of it would not stand the test of the investigation, a newspaper vindication would be of little avail; but as immense pains have been taken to disseminate these counterfeit letters, I conceived it a justice due to my own character and to posterity to disown them in explicit terms; and this I did in a letter directed to the Secretary of State, to be filed in his office, the day on which I closed my administration. This letter has since been published in the gazettes by the head of that department." *

This letter is now on file among the papers in the Department of State, is written by Timothy Pickering, and merely signed by the President. I give it in full:

PHILADELPHIA, 3 March, 1797.

DEAR SIR:—At the conclusion of my public employments, I have thought it expedient to notice the publication of certain forged letters, which first appeared in the year 1777, and were obtruded upon the public as mine. They are said by the editor to have been found in a small portmanteau that I had left in the care of my mulatto servant, named Billy, who, it is pretended, was taken prisoner at Fort Lee, 1776.

The period when these letters were first printed, will be recollected, and what were the impressions they

---

* *Washington to William Gordon*, 13 October, 1797. Gordon proposed to republish in England the two volumes of genuine letters, with a few which he had copied during the war.

were

were intended to produce on the public mind. It was then supposed to be of some consequence to strike at the integrity of the motives of the American Commander in Chief, and to paint his inclinations as at variance with his professions and his duty. Another crisis in the affairs of America having occurred, the same weapon has been resorted to, to wound my character and deceive the people.

The letters in question have the dates, addresses and signatures here following:

"New York, June 12th, 1776. To Mr. *Lund Washington*, at Mount Vernon, Fairfax County, Virginia."
"G. W."

"To *John Parke Custis*, Esq., at the Hon. Benedict Calvert's, Esq., Mount Airy, Maryland," "June 18th, 1776."
"G. W."

"New York, July 8th, 1776. To Mr. *Lund Washington*, at Mount Vernon, Fairfax County, Virginia."
"G. W."

"New York, July 16th, 1876. To Mr. *Lund Washington*, etc."
"G. W."

"New York, July 15th, 1776. To Mr. *Lund Washington*, etc."
"G. W."

"New York, July 22d, 1776. To Mr. *Lund Washington*, etc."
"G. W."

"June 24th, 1776. To Mrs. *Washington*." "G. W."

At the time when these letters first appeared, it was notorious to the army immediately under my command, and particularly to the gentlemen attached to my person, that my mulatto man *Billy* had never been one moment in the power of the enemy. It is also a fact that no part of my baggage or any of my attendants were captured during the whole course of the war. These well-known facts made it unnecessary, during the war, to call the public attention to the forgery, by any express declaration of mine; and a firm reliance

on

on my fellow-citizens, and the abundant proofs they gave of their confidence in me, rendered it alike unnecessary to take any formal notice of the revival of the imposition during my civil administration. But as I cannot know how soon a more serious event may succeed to that which will this day take place, I have thought it a duty that I owe to myself, to my country, and to truth, now to detail the circumstances above recited, and to add my solemn declaration, that the letters herein described are a base forgery, and that I never saw or heard of them until they appeared in print.

The present letter I commit to your care, and desire it may be deposited in the office of the department of State, as a testimony of the truth to the present generation and to posterity.

Accept, I pray you, the sincere esteem and affectionate regard of,

Dear Sir,
Your obedient
G? Washington.

Timothy Pickering,
    Secretary of State.

This letter, prefaced by a little note from Pickering, was sent to the gazettes, and widely printed throughout the country. Such a characterization would, of course, discredit the volume which contained the denounced epistles, and destroy the sale of the book, while disturbing the plans of its compilers. Did they call in and suppress the unsold copies? Did the publishers make any explanation for having been led into publishing the collection? Was a reparation made to the injured sensitiveness of the now retired President? If any of these acts were performed, I have been able to find

find no record of them, save in one instance. In a few copies of the Epistles I find pasted into the front a reprint of the Washington-Pickering letter, printed in octavo form, and probably designed to protect the seller in case any question should arise, rather than disabuse the misplaced confidence of the buyer in the genuineness of his purchase. When I came across this leaf in one copy of the *Epistles* in my father's collection, I thought it unique, and it was long before I came across another. In the catalogue of Henry Steven's sale of 1872 mention is made of "the rare page printed to match" the book, and the catalogue adds. "This ought to have ended the matter, but it did not, for to this day there are writers who from choice or warped moral vision give credit to lies rather than to truth."

The volume of *Epistles, Domestic, Confidential, and Official*, was reprinted in England in 1796 by the Rivington's, and was noticed in the *Monthly Review* :*

"We believe that the *whole* of what are here entitled 'Epistles, domestic, confidential, and official, from General Washington,' are only a republication of the letters which were notoriously fabricated and first published in London, soon after the commencement of the American war, for the purpose of engaging the people of this country to approve the continuance of it. We ought, however, to except those materials which compose the *Appendix*, and which have been copied from newspapers, etc,, in order, no doubt, to reflect some credit on those that were forged; and forged, undoubtedly, by a Mr. V——, then a young Episcopal clergyman,

---

* *The Monthly Review or Literary Journal enlarged*, vol. xxi, 475.

clergyman, who came from New York, in order to make his fortune *here*, in the character of a *Loyalist*."

A word as to the fabricator of these letters. The "young Episcopal clergyman" suggested by the *Monthly Review*, was probably the Rev. John Vardill, a graduate of King's College, who had gone to England in 1774 to take Holy Orders, and had remained there, although appointed assistant rector of Trinity Church in New York. It is known that he was in the employ of the government, and wielded a ready pen in the service of his masters, some poetical satires on the Whigs being attributed to him. Trumbull, in "McFingal," wrote:

> "In Vardill, that poetic zealot,
> I view a lawn bedizen'd Prelate;
> While mitres fall, as 'tis their duty,
> On heads of Chandler and Auchmuty."

I confess, I should dislike to believe, except on the plainest proof, that one in Holy Orders could stoop so low as to utter forged papers with a view to deliberately injure the reputation of another man. Party enthusiasm too often has degenerated into such immorality, and men who would not consciously violate truth or decency under any other circumstances have been known in factional fights to say and do what the simple primer of morality would condemn as wrong. Even the plea of necessity can not excuse such wanderings from the line of truth and justice. It is only recently that we were treated to the humiliating spectacle of a great national party, claiming to be a party

party of moral ideas, banking upon a set of forged utterances that, impossible on their face, were so easily shown to be false as to give rise to a feeling of wonderment that their use could even have suggested itself to a reasoning and reasonable creature.*

Apart, however, from any such moral objection to laying these forged letters at the door of a clergyman, his lack of a knowledge of Washington's habits of thought and ways of living, would offer a forcible argument against his having composed them. Vardill went to England in 1774, as a young man of about 22, and did not return again to America. It is possible that the materials might have been furnished to him by some other loyalist, or by a number of loyalists, in England; but even then it would be difficult for one, a perfect stranger to Washington and to Virginia, to have turned out so clever a performance—for it is undeniably clever, even the punctuation being characteristic of the supposed writer.

It is far more probable that the fabricator was from Virginia, and as Washington says, some one possessed of a knowledge of the family and life at Mount Vernon. Fortunately we are not entirely without foundation for making a conjecture, as we have important evidence, giving probably Washington's own suspicions, contained

* The New York *Evening Post*, which did excellent service in running down and exposing these forgeries, pointed out in its issue of 14 October, 1889, that the scheme of manufacturing sham extracts from English papers for political purposes was practised by the first Napoleon. He wrote to Fouché, 28 August, 1804: "The notes you have sent me upon the powerlessness of Russia are written by a man of sense. Publish them in a newspaper as translated from an English paper; choose the name of one that is little known." *Lanfrey*, ii, 146.

in a letter from Col. Tench Tilghman, then in the military family of Washington, and well known to possess his confidence: "The letters published under General Washington's signature are not genuine. They are intended for the purposes you mention. He suspects Jack Randolph for the author, as the letters contain a knowledge of his family affairs that none but a Virginian could be acquainted with. The sentiments are noble, and such as the General himself often expresses. I have heard him declare a thousand times, and he does it every day in the most public company, that independence was farthest of anything from his thoughts, and that he never entertained the idea until he plainly saw that absolute conquest was the aim, and unconditional submission the terms which Great Britian meant to grant." *Tench Tilghman to James Tilghman, Valley Forge*, 24 April 1778. And as further proof may be cited a MS. note on the New York leaflet, in the handwriting of Du Simitiere: "Spurious: wrote in London by a Mr. Randolph of Virginia."

Apart from these data we are able to appeal to some internal evidences which seem to point to Randolph as the writer. He approaches accuracy when detailing matters or impressions that occurred prior to November, 1775, when he sailed for England, although he is sadly mixed in dates. For example Washington's anxiety that his wife should undergo inoculation may reasonably have been shown in his letters to her in the fall of 1775, when he invited her to join him in the camp at Cambridge. Randolph was intimate with Mrs. Washington and may have seen some of these letters, and thus

thus obtained the idea of that which is included among these spurious letters. So also, as regards the reasons that induced Washington to accept the command, which are detailed with historical accuracy, and make an interesting addition to what may be gathered from other and clearly authentic sources.* He may have gathered this information from Mrs. Washington, from one of the correspondents of the general's in Virginia, or from his son, Edmund Randolph, who served in Washington's family from August to November 1775. Indeed, much of that knowledge of what occupied Washington's thoughts, (and it is curious to note how happily at times the forger has anticipated what the general did write to persons who would not have suffered the letters to become public in their generation,) may have been based upon what Edmund had written him in these few months of military experience. To the members of his family Washington was communicative, for he trusted them implicitly, and I do not find a single instance in which this trust was misplaced. Certainly by the end of August, 1775, the evils of the temporary expedients and dilatory action of Congress had been felt, and had been freely discussed by the general with his aids—with what freedom his letters to Reed proved. There were many sources from which Randolph could have obtained information of what was going on, but none more likely than from his son.

The little personality, touching a conversation with "a friend, now most unjustly as unwisely, driven from

---

* **Appendix.**

his

his friends and his home"* is not without its value, for Randolph maintained his loyalty to the king, and was forced to seek safety on board the ship where Dunmore was plotting against the lives and property of those whom he had been sent to govern, and whom, there is evidence to show, he had wantonly sacrificed to his own selfish aims, pleading the safety of the State and the interest of his king. Another line of evidence is the strong belief, shown throughout these letters, in the idea of a reconciliation between the rebellious colonies and the mother country. That, also, was an article of Randolph's belief, and, as Mr. Conway suggests, Jefferson regarded his departure for England somewhat in the light of a mission.† "Looking with fondness towards a reconciliation with Great Britain, I cannot help hoping you may be able to contribute toward expediting the good work." *Jefferson to John Randolph*, 25 August, 1775. In the manuscripts preserved in Drayton House, Northamptonshire, in the possession of the family of Lord George Germaine, is one unsigned, dated 4 August, 1780, and endorsed, "Mr. Randolph's plan of accommodation"—undoubtedly drawn up and submitted to the British ministry by the loyalist refugee from Virginia. How dearly he paid for harboring such a hope and irrevocably attaching himself to the loyalist side, with the hated Dunmore as the type and leader, history relates, though it has preserved almost nothing that relates to the king's attorney, long the ablest lawyer in Virginia,

---

* Letter, 16 July 1776, *Post*.
† Conway, *Omitted Chapters of History*, 20.

save

save this fatal step. Randolph is said to have lived in London on an annuity of £100, and dying in 1784 of a broken heart, expressed the wish that he might find a resting place in Virginia, whose cause he had deserted nine years before.

And finally should be noted the opinions expressed on the leaders in Virginia politics. Under the colonial rule all the offices of state were at the gift of the king, or of his agent the Governor. In distributing this patronage, the leading idea was to bestow it upon such men of influence or property as would strengthen the royal power in the colony. The Governor, the Attorney general, and the Privy council of the Governor, were thus emblems of royal prerogative, as opposed to the House of Burgesses, which represented the popular element—the home or local influence. Almost unconsciously there sprung up a line separating the holders of the higher offices from the popular branch, a line difficult to trace or define, but none the less dividing the active political forces into two factions—for they do not deserve the title of parties. The former may be called the aristocrats, and the latter the republicans, but it is impossible to say in precise terms wherein their difference lay, or to allot to either party definite leaders. Patrick Henry, Thomas Jefferson, Mercer and Page, may be cited among the liberal or republican element, while the Nelsons, the Randolphs, the Byrds, the Lees, Corbins and Carters, were on the other side. So that it is quite natural to find little sympathy among the latter for Patrick Henry and the new constitution, and a word of praise for the Lees, and the new council.

In

In the light of these evidences it would not be right to assert positively that the fabricator of these letters was John Randolph, the last king's attorney general of Virginia; but they offer reasonable proof tending to show that he might have written them.

The letters are now reprinted from the London edition of 1777, and differ somewhat from the version I have given in my *Writings of Washington*, not only in verbal detail, but notably in correcting the curious alteration of dates occasioned by Rivington. Some temporary interest was revived the last spring in these letters by a mention of them in a political speech arising from the Parnell Commission. Sir William Harcourt adduced an historical parallel to the Pigott forgeries in these forged letters pronounced against General Washington.

The letters have some historical importance, and being out of print, and the original issues of some rarity, I determined upon this republication, with notes and illustrations taken from the genuine writings of Washington. I have added some contemporary sketches of Washington, and other material gathered from sources not likely to be discovered by the student. There may be some doubt of the value of these records as true descriptions, and just characterizations; but their antiquarian interest is something in their favor, and to a student of Washington's career and character, no record is to be laid aside as worthless. A casual sentence penned by the greatest scoundrel in ministerial pay, a few words written by a friend, will often be found to contain what is of vital moment in determining a question

of

of history, or a phase of the workings of Washington's mind. This is my excuse for again giving to the world what at first thought might better be left in forgetfulness. It may also be added that for the first time since these fabrications first saw the light, they are laid before the public in their true character, as forged or spurious letters.

WORTHINGTON CHAUNCEY FORD.

Washington, 30 October, 1889.

BIBLIOGRAPHY.

Letters / from / General Washington. / To several of his Friends in the / year 1776. / In which are set forth / a fairer and fuller view of / American Politics, / than ever yet transpired, / or the Public could be made acquainted with / through any other channel.
  London : Printed for J. Bew, No. 28, Paternoster-Row. M,DCC,LXXVII.

8vo. pp. 73.

The arrangement of the letters in this first issue differs somewhat from that of the American editions:

1. To Lund Washington, 12 June, 1776.
2.   John Parke Custis, 18 June, 1776.
3.   Lady Washington, 24 June, 1776.
4.   Lund Washington, 16 July, 1776.
5.   Lund Washington, 8 July, 1777 (*sic*).
6.   Lund Washington, 15 July, 1776.
7.   Lund Washington, 22 July, 1776.

LETTERS

FROM

GENERAL WASHINGTON,

To several of his FRIENDS in the Year 1776.

IN WHICH ARE SET FORTH,

A FAIRER and FULLER VIEW

OF

AMERICAN POLITICKS,

THAN EVER YET TRANSPIRED,

Or the PUBLIC could be made acquainted with through any other Channel.

TOGETHER WITH

The Reverend Mr. JACOB DUCHE's (late Chaplain to the Congress) LETTER to Mr. WASHINGTON, and an ANSWER to it, by Mr. JOHN PARKE, a Lieutenant-Colonel in Mr. Washington's Army.

PRINTED IN THE YEAR 1778.

In the New York issue of 1778 the order was as follows:

1. To Lund Washington, 12 June, 1776.
2. John Parke Custis, 18 June, 1776.
3. Lund Washington, 8 July, 1776.*
4. Lund Washington, 16 July, 1776. †
5. Lund Washington, 15 July, 1776.
6. Lund Washington, 22 July, 1776.
7. Mrs. Washington, 24 July, 1776.

Letters from General Washington to several of his Friends, in June and July, 1776, In which is set Forth, an Interesting View of American Politics, at that All-Important Period.

Philadelphia: Republished at the Federal Press, 1795.

8vo, pp. 44.

Epistles Domestic, Confidential, and Official, from General Washington. Written about the Commencement of the American Contest, when he entered on the Command of the Army of the United States. With an Interesting Series of his Letters, particularly to the British Admirals Arbuthnot and Digby, to Gen. Sir Henry Clinton, Lord Cornwallis, Sir Guy Carleton, Marquis de la Fayette, etc., etc. To Ben-

---

* This letter is that dated the 16th July in the English edition.

† This is the letter bearing date July 8th in the English edition. These same errors were reproduced in all later editions.

jamin

jamin Harrison, Esq, Speaker of the House of Delegates in Virginia, to Admiral the Count de Grasse, General Sullivan, respecting an attack of New York; including many applications and addresses presented to him with his answers; Orders and Instructions, on important occasions, to his Aids de Camp, etc. etc. etc. None of which have been printed in the two volumes published a few months ago.

New York: Printed by G. Robinson, corner of William and John Streets, and J. Bull, No. 115 Cherry Street, and sold by James Rivington, No. 156 Pearl Street. M,DCC,XCVI.

8vo, *pp.* xiv., 303. Portrait engraved after Savage by Rollinson. The letters to p. 66 are spurious.

Same title. New York: Printed. London: Reprinted for F. and C. Rivington. 1796.
8vo, *pp.* xvi., 303. No portrait.

Official Letters / to the Honorable / American Congress, / Written during the War between the / United Colonies and Great Britain, / by his Excellency, / George Washington, / Commander in Chief of the Continental Forces, / now / President of the United States. / Copied, by special Permission, from the Original Papers preserved / in the office of the Secretary of State, Philadelphia.

London: Printed for G. G. and J. Robinson, B. and J. White, T. Cadell and W. Davies, W. Otridge

Otridge and Son, *J. Debrett, R. Faulder, and T. Egerton*. 1795.

2 *vols,*, '8*vo*, *pp.* viii., 364; 384. The last letter printed is dated December 31, 1778.

Same title. *Boston: Printed by Manning & Loring*, for S. Hall, W. Spotswood, J. White, Thomas and Andrews, D. West, E. Larkin, W. P. Blake, and J. West. 1795.

2 *vols.*, 8*vo*, *pp.* vi., 340, 356. A second Boston edition was issued in 1796, the collation being the same, with the addition, however, of a portrait of the President, engraved by S. Hill, from a portrait by Edward Savage.

Same title. *New York: Printed and sold by Samuel Campbell: No. 124 Pearl Street.* M,DCC,XCVI. 2*vols.*, 8*vo.*, *pp.* [2] 276; 311.

LETTERS

FROM

GENERAL WASHINGTON,

To several of his FRIENDS in the Year 1776.

IN WHICH ARE SET FORTH

A FAIRER and FULLER VIEW OF

AMERICAN POLITICS.

THAN EVER YET TRANSPIRED,

Or the PUBLIC could be made acquainted with through any other Channel.

LONDON:

Printed for J. BEW, No. 28, *Pater-Noster Row.*
M.DCC.LXXVII.

(Price One Shilling and Sixpence.)

TO MR. LUND WASHINGTON, AT MOUNT VERNON, FAIRFAX COUNTY, VIRGINIA.*

NEW YORK, 12 JUNE, 1776.

DEAR LUND,

Though I wrote to you but a very few days ago, and have nothing new of much moment to communicate, I cannot deny myself the comfort of unburthening my mind to you, whenever I have a little leisure, amid the thousand anxieties and disquietudes that almost distract me. I know the goodness of your heart, and that you will attend to me with indulgence and sympathy, though it be not in your power any otherwise to afford me relief. There cannot, in the nature of things, be a situation so truly irksome to an ingenuous mind, as the being perpetually obliged

---

*"Lund Washington, born 1737, died 1796, was the son of Townshend Washington, of 'Greenhill,' Choptauck, (who married Elizabeth Lund) and was thus a great-grandson of Lawrence (the immigrant) brother of the General's great-grandfather. Lund W. married Elizabeth Foote in 1782, by whom he left no issue. He managed Mount Vernon for twenty-five years, retiring in 1785, residing thereafter at 'Hayfield,' an estate of 1200 acres about five miles from Mount Vernon. Washington parted from him reluctantly. In 1778 he wrote that his (Lund's) wages were 'totally inadequate to [his] trouble and services,' and insisted on his having a share of the produce of the estate of more value than a payment in depreciated currency."
—From Moncure D. Conway's notes in '*George Washington and Mount Vernon*,' published by the Long Island *Historical Society*, 1889.

to act a part foreign to our true feelings; yet this, alas! as you know, is, and must be, my lot. I wear a countenance dressed in the calm serenity of perfect confidence, whilst my heart is corroded with infinite apprehensions, and I have no bosom friend near me, to whom I dare lay it open. Tell me, Lund, for you have long been privy to my most secret thoughts,—trusting to thy native candor, I have never hesitated to lay my heart bare and open to thy inspection; tell me then, am I, do you think, more subject to fears than other men? For I will not conceal it from you, that, at this moment, I feel myself a very coward. Do not mistake me;—I thank my God, I have never yet known what it was to fear for any personal danger that might befal me. I am not afraid to die—why should I? I am afraid only to die with infamy and disgrace. And, if I am afraid so to die, need I tell you that I am ten thousand times more afraid to live, like Lucifer, a fallen Angel. No, Lund, that were too much; betide what will, I cannot, and I will not survive either my misfortunes, or my disgraces. Heaven, that knows my heart, knows how truly I love my country;* and that I embarked in this arduous enterprise on the purest motives. But, we have overshot our mark:

---

* The sentences "Do not mistake me" etc., to "knows how truly I love my country" were printed in the *Daily Advertiser* (N. Y.), 11 September, 95.

we

we have grasped at things beyond our reach : it is
impossible we should succeed ; and, I cannot with
truth, say that I am sorry for it ; because I am far
from being sure that we deserve to succeed. That
the British ministry had meditated schemes fatal
to the liberties of America ; and that, if we had
not opposed their first efforts to impose taxes on
us, without our consent, we might have bid adieu
to every idea of constitutional security hereafter I
have not a doubt. Nay, I am so thoroughly persuaded of the unworthiness of their designs, and
of the duty of every honest American to oppose
them, that, dissatisfied as I am with my situation,
were it to do over again, I would rather be even as
I am than tamely crouch, whilst chains were fast-
ening round my neck.* For there is not, in my
estimation, so vile a thing upon earth as a human
being who, having once enjoyed liberty, can
patiently bear to see it taken from him. I would
and I will die ten thousand deaths, rather than be
this thing myself. On these principles, and these

---

* " When the councils of the British nation had formed a plan for enslav-
ing America, and depriving her sons of their most sacred and invaluable
privileges, against the clearest remonstrances of the constitution, of justice,
and of truth, and, to execute their schemes, had appealed to the sword, I
esteemed it my duty to take part in the contest, and more especially on account of my being called thereto by the unsolicited suffrages of the representatives of a free people ; wishing for no other reward than that arising
from a conscientious discharge of the important trust, and that my services
might contribute to the establishment of freedom and peace, upon a permanent foundation, and merit the applause of my countrymen, and every virtuous citizen." *Washington's reply to an Address from the General Assembly
of Massachusetts*, March, 1776.

only,

only, I first took up arms: but my misfortune, and the true source of all my uneasiness is, that though in good policy, as well as honor, these ought to be the principles of every American, I have long ago discovered, they are not. And it is on this account alone, that I dread our defeat. Our want of skill, our want of ammunition, in short, our want of almost everything which an army ought to have, are all, no doubt, exceedingly against us: but, they are all nothing to our want of virtue.— Unused to the many arts and devices, by which designing men carry their points, I unwillingly listened to my own apprehensions, when early in the first Congress, I thought I saw a tendency to measures which I never could approve of. I reasoned myself, however, out of my fears, with no ordinary reproach on my own meanness, in having given way to suspicions, which could not be true, unless we had men amongst ourselves more flagitious than even those we were opposing. At length, however, when a continental army came to be voted for, my fears returned with redoubled force: for then, for the first time, I clearly saw our aims reached farther than we cared to avow. It was carried with an unanimity that really astonished me; because, I knew many who voted for it, were as averse to the independency of America, as I was. And they even ridiculed me for my apprehensions on that account; and, indeed,

deed, when they suggested that Great Britain, seeing us apparently determined to risque every thing rather than that they should tax us, would never think of engaging in a civil war with us, which must necessarily cost her more than even America could repay her, I could not but hope, that I was mistaken; and that our military preparations might be a good political movement. In one thing, however, we all agreed, that, as the forces were chiefly to be raised in New-England, it would be extremely rash and imprudent in the southern delegates to leave them in the possession of so formidable a power without any check. I need not tell you, that it was this consideration which, if I am to be credited, sorely against my will, determined me to accept of the command of this army. We set out with bad omens; I was mistrustful of them in every thing; and they were taught to look upon me with jealousy. This soon manifested itself in forming them to any thing like decent discipline. But I have, long ago, pestered you more than enough with complaints on this head.—I knew not, however, certainly, that I had been appointed to this high station only to be disgraced and ruined, till about the middle of the latter end of last February.* When, contrary to

---

* "I found a mixed multitude of people here, under very little discipline, order, or government." *Washington to the President of Congress*, 27 July, 1775. "From my own experience I can easily judge of your difficulties to

my

my wishes, I found it necessary that we should come to open hostilities against our fellow-subjects in the ministerial army: doubtless, common prudence required that when we did attempt it, we should, if possible, do it speedily and effectually. And, having all the reason in the world to believe that large armies would be sent against us early in the summer, I resolved, cost what it would, to cut off those already here, which would have given us such infinite advantages over any future reinforcements that might be sent. And this I believe was easily in our power; but, as I have already told you, nothing is to be done with our New England allies, unless they are let into all your secrets. I could not advance a step without communicating my intentions to the gentlemen in the civil depart-

---

introduce order and discipline into troops, who have from their infancy imbibed ideas of the most contrary kind. It would be far beyond the compass of a letter for me to describe the situation of things here on my arrival. Perhaps you will only be able to judge of it from my assuring you, that mine must be a portrait at full length of what you have had in miniature." *Washington to Schuyler*, 26 July, 1775. "There has been so many great and capital errors and abuses to rectify, so many examples to make, and so little inclination in the officers of inferior rank to contribute their aid to accomplish this work, that my life has been nothing else (*since I came here*), *but* one continued round of *annoyance and fatigue;* in short no pecuniary *recompense* could induce me to undergo what *I have, especially* as I expect by shewing so little *countenance* to irregularities and publick *abuses to* render myself obnoxious to a *greater* part of these people." *Washington to Richard Henry Lee*, 29 August, 1775. "Could I have foreseen what I have, and am likely to experience, no consideration upon earth could have induced me to accept this command. A regiment or any subordinate department would have been accompanied with ten times the satisfaction, and perhaps the honor." *Washington to Joseph Reed*, 28 November, 1775.

ment;

ment; a thing ever ruinous in war.* It soon got wind, as I had foreseen; and it appeared, that the General of the enemy was apprized of my design. Still, however, I persevered in my purpose; which, in spite of all his care and caution, I was confident must succeed, and reduce him to the utmost extremity. But (as every military man must know) so capital a blow was not to be struck without the loss both of many men, and much property! For my design was, if they would not surrender by an

---

*"I can bear to hear of reputed or real errors. The man who wishes to stand well in the opinion of others must do this; because he is thereby enabled to correct his faults, or remove prejudices which are imbibed against him. For this reason, I shall thank you for giving me the opinions of the world upon such points as you know me to be interested in; for, as I have but one capital object in view, I could wish to make my conduct coincide with the wish of mankind, as far as I can consistently; I mean, without departing from that great line of duty, which, though hid under a cloud for some time, from a peculiarity of circumstances may nevertheless bear a scrutiny. My constant attention to the great and perplexing objects which continually rise to my view, absorbs all lesser considerations, and indeed scarcely allows me time to reflect that there is such a body in existence as the General Court of this colony, but when I am reminded of it by a committee; nor can I, upon recollection, discover in what instances (I wish they would be more explicit) I have been inattentive to, or slighted them. They could not, surely, conceive that there was a propriety in unbosoming the secret of an army to them; that it was necessary to ask their opinion in throwing up an intrenchment, forming a batallion, etc, etc." *Washington to Joseph Reed*, 14 January, 1776.

"Your acknowledgment of my attention to the civil constitution of this colony, whilst active in the line of my department, also demands my grateful thanks. A regard to every Provincial institution, where not incompatible with the common interest, I hold a principle of duty and of policy, and it shall ever form a part of my conduct. Had I not learnt this before, the happy experience of the advantages resulting from a friendly intercourse with your honorable body, their ready and willing concurrence to aid and to counsel whenever called upon in cases of difficulty and emergency, would have taught me the useful lesson." *Washington's reply to an address of the General Assembly of Massachusetts*, March, 1776.

honorable

honorable capitulation to burn the town about their ears, and so rush in, and cut them off in their attempts to escape to the ships. And this, with our superiority of numbers, we certainly could have effected; though no doubt, it would have been a bloody business, if they had not surrendered, as I think they would. But when, as I was obliged, I laid this before the Council and Representatives, they not only found a thousand objections to it, but absolutely restrained me; and I could not have got a man that would have gone on what they called so desperate a scheme. Hence was I under a necessity of proceeding in the poor, slow, and unsoldier-like manner, which not only gave them an opportunity to escape, but has taught them to despise us. There is no forming an idea of the importance of such a stroke at that juncture. If anything upon earth could have made America independent and glorious, that was the golden opportunity. I confess to you, I had worked my imagination up to such a pitch of high expectation, that my disappointment has dispirited me in a manner I never can recover. For, from that moment, I have despaired of our ever doing any thing truly great. Any little gleams of success, or fairer prospects we have since had, serve but to make our inferiority the more conspicuous. For what incidents can fall out to aggrandize us, who can be made great only by great and spirited efforts,

efforts, when we have shewn that we wanted both the understanding and the virtue to purchase to ourselves immortal glory on better and cheaper terms than ever we can hope hereafter to have it? But, the worst remains yet to be told. Some of those very men who were the most forward to thwart me in this measure, had discovered a different way of thinking on other occasions: and, I am persuaded that were the question put to them now, as to this city, and the southern regiments, I should not hear a dissentient voice. But let me spare you.*

---

* Congress, and individual members of that body, did not hesitate to make suggestions to Washington on military matters, to his no small discomfort, as a suggestion from such a source might be regarded as an order. On October 3d, 1775, Congress had adopted a resolution authorizing Washington to offer an encouragement to the soldiers in case of an attack upon Boston, but a council of the general officers decided that an attack at that time was not practicable. The idea, however, was ever present in Washington's mind, and was one of the questions submitted to the committee from Congress that visited the camp in October. Lynch, one of this committee, wrote to Washington in November: "I mean not to anticipate your determination, but only to approve your design to hover like an eagle over your prey, always ready to pounce upon it when the proper time comes. I have not forgot your proposition relative to that city; I try to pave the way for it, and wait for the season, as you do." Finally on December 22d, Congress passed a secret resolve that " if General Washington and his council of war should be of opinion, that a successful attack may be made on the troops in Boston, he do it in any manner he may think expedient, notwithstanding the town and property in it may be destroyed." In acknowledging this resolution Washington gave assurance that he would attempt to put it in execution " the first moment I see a probability of success, and in such a way as a council of officers shall think most likely to produce it; but if this should not happen as soon as you may expect, or my wishes prompt to, request that Congress will be pleased to advert to my situation, and do me the justice to believe, that circumstances, and no want of inclination are the cause of delay." *Washington to the President of Congress*, 4 January, 1776. "Could I have foreseen the difficulties, which have come upon us; could I have known, that such a backwardness would have been discovered in the old

After all this, you will again, I doubt not, as you often have, ask me, why I continue in a situation so disagreeable to me? I wish you had forborne this question, the truth being, that I neither am

---

soldiers to the service, all the generals upon earth should not have convinced me of the propriety of delaying an attack upon Boston till this time. When it can now be attempted, I will not undertake to say; but this much I will answer for, that no opportunity can present itself earlier than my wishes." *Washington to Joseph Reed*, 14 January, 1776. The want of powder was a serious check upon any operations, offensive or defensive, and proved the most perplexing problem that Washington was called upon to solve. Again and again did he call upon Congress and the separate colonies for a supply of this most necessary article, and disappointed in obtaining it, saw himself condemned to inactivity. "Why will not Congress forward part of the powder made in your province? They seem to look upon this as the season for action, but will not furnish the means. I will not blame them. I dare say the demands upon them are greater than they can supply. The cause must be starved till our resources are greater, or more certain within ourselves." *Washington to Reed*, 10 February, 1776. At last, in February, he thought the conditions favorable for making an attack, as a broad expanse of ice afforded a comparatively safe passage from Dorchester Point and Roxbury to the city. In spite of an army much reduced in number, and in spite of having no powder with which to begin a regular cannonade and bombardment, Washington, on the 16th, laid the plan of assault before his general officers, and to his mortification it was almost unanimously disapproved. Washington acquiesced in the decision with reluctance; for "from a thorough conviction of attempting something against the ministerial troops before a reinforcement should arrive, and while we were favored with the ice, I was not only ready, but willing and desirous of making the assault, under a firm hope, if the men would have stood by me, of a favorable issue, notwithstanding the enemy's advantage of ground, artillery, etc." *Washington to the President of Congress*, 18 February, 1776. And to Joseph Reed he wrote on the 26th: "I proposed it [an assault] in council; but behold, tho' we had been waiting all the year for this favorable event, the enterprise was thought too dangerous. Perhaps it was; perhaps the irksomeness of my situation led me to undertake more than could be warranted by prudence. I did not think so, and I am sure yet, that the enterprise, if it had been undertaken with resolution, must have succeeded; without it any would fail; but it is now at an end, and I am preparing to take post on Dorchester, to try if the enemy will be so kind as to come out to us."

As to a rumored intention on the part of Washington to burn New York, see his letter of August 23d, 1776, to the New York Convention.

able,

able, nor very willing to answer it. My resolution to hold it out as long as I can is dictated by my feelings, which I neither can describe to you, nor wholly justify on paper; but which, however, I find it impossible for me to disregard.—The eyes of all America, perhaps, of Europe, of the world, are fixed on me. It has been our policy, (and, at the time, I thought it well founded) to hold out false lights to the world. There are not an hundred men in America that know our true situation; three-fourths of the Congress itself are ignorant of it;—yourself excepted, there lives not a man at all acquainted with my peculiar circumstances. The world looks upon us as in possession of an army all animated with the pure flame of liberty, and determined to die rather than not be free. It is in possession of proofs, that it is so, under my own hand:—I have always so spoken of it, and I still do.* But, you know how remote, in my judg-

---

* "It is in vain to expect that any more than a trifling part of this army will again engage in the service on the encouragement offered by Congress. When men find that their townsmen and companions are receiving twenty, thirty, and more dollars for a few months' service, which is truly the case, it cannot be expected without using compulsion; and to force them into the service would answer no valuable purpose. When men are irritated, and their passions inflamed, they fly hastily and cheerfully to arms; but, after the first emotions are over, to expect among such people as compose the bulk of an army, that they are influenced by any other principles than those of interest, is to look for what never did, and I fear never will happen; the Congress will deceive themselves, therefore, if they expect it. A soldier, reasoned with upon the goodness of the cause he is engaged in, and the inestimable rights he is contending for, hears you with patience, and acknowledges the truth of your observations, but adds that it is of no more

ment,

ment, all this is from the truth, though I am not sure that there is another man in the army, besides myself, that thinks so. I should guess, however, that there are many. But, tied up as my own mouth is, it is little to be wondered at that theirs are so too, at least to me.—Thus circumstanced, can you point out a way in which it is possible for me to resign, just now as it were, on the eve of

---

importance to him than to others. The officer makes you the same reply, with this further remark, that his pay will not support him, and he cannot ruin himself and family to serve his country, when every member of the community is equally interested, and benefitted by his labors. The few, therefore, who act upon principles of disinterestedness, comparatively speaking, are no more than a drop in the ocean." *Washington to Congress*, 24 September, 1776.

"Notwithstanding all the public virtue which is ascribed to these people, there is no nation under the sun (that I ever came across) pay greater adoration to money than they do." *Washington to Joseph Reed*, 10 February, 1776.

"Such a dearth of public spirit, and want of virtue, such stock-jobbing, and fertility in all the low arts to obtain advantages of one kind or another, in this great change of military arrangement, I never saw before, and pray God I may never be witness to again." *Washington to Joseph Reed*, 28 November, 1776.

"I know—but to declare it, unless to a friend, may be an argument of vanity—the integrity of my own heart. I know the unhappy predicament I stand in; I know that much is expected of me; I know, that without men, without arms, without ammunition, without anything fit for the accommodation of a soldier, little is to be done; and, which is mortifying, I know that I cannot stand justified to the world without exposing my own weakness, and injuring the cause by declaring my wants, which I am determined not to do, further than unavoidable necessity brings every man acquainted with them." *Washington to Joseph Reed*, 10 February, 1776.

"To have the eyes of the whole continent fixed with anxious expectation of hearing some great event, and to be restrained in every military operation for want of the necessary means of carrying it on, is not very pleasing, especially as the means used to conceal my weakness from the enemy, conceals it also from our friends, and adds to their wonder." *Washington to the President of Congress*, 18 February, 1776.

action,

action, without imputation of cowardice? There is no such way. Besides, diffident and desponding as I am, how do I know, that it is not so with those we have to oppose? they certainly have reason. The events of war depend on a thousand minutiæ, without the ken of a mere bystander. I know not that the commander of the armies of the low-countries, could his heart have been read as you do mine, had not the same fears, and the same causes for them that I have. You learn not this from the history; nor was it to be expected you should. Yet, he succeeded at last. And, who knows, what an over-ruling providence, who often brings about the greatest revolutions by the most unlikely means, may intend for America? If it be the will of God, that America should be independent of Great Britain, and that this be the reason for it, even I and these unhopeful men around may not be thought unworthy instruments in his hands. And, should we succeed, we are heroes, and immortalized beyond even those of former times. Whereas disgrace only, and intolerable infamy await our retreat.* In this persuasion, I resolve to

---

*I solemnly protest that a pecuniary reward of twenty thousand pounds a year would not induce me to undergo what I do; and after all, perhaps, to lose my character, as it is impossible, under such a variety of distressing circumstances, to conduct matters agreeably to public expectations, or even to the expectation of those who employ me, as they will not make proper allowances for the difficulties their own errors have occasioned." *Washington to his brother*, 19 November, 1776.

go on, contented, with the glorious King William, to save my country, or die in the last ditch. I am, my dear Lund, your Faithful Friend and Servant,

G. W.

TO JOHN PARKE CUSTIS, ESQ., AT THE HON. BENEDICT CALVERT'S, ESQ., MOUNT AIRY, MARYLAND.*

18 June, 1776.

My Very Dear Jack,

You have exceedingly obliged me by your letter which I received by yesterday's post. It discovers an attention to the great affairs now carrying on, and an information concerning them, which I own to you, I had not given you credit for. Your youth and inexperience pleaded your excuse: and though you gave me no opportunity to praise you for any active exertions, I paid you no ordinary compliments, in my own mind, for your modesty in forbearing to meddle with things which it was no reproach to you to confess, were out of your reach. Considering your rank, fortune and education, whenever it is proper for you to come forward on the theatre, it must not be any underpart that you act. You are, therefore, certainly in the right to decline taking any part at all, till you are fit for a first and a leading character. And you have my full and perfect approbation of your resolution to

---

*John Parke Custis was born in November, 1754. He died in October, 1781, of a camp fever.

persist in your purpose, for the present, not to accept of any rank, either civil or military. I see your anxiety, lest the present opportunity for signalizing your just love for your country should, by your not unnecessary cautions, be suffered to slip by you, unimproved. Your ardor is commendable; and far be it from me to discourage in you a spirit I so much love. But, whilst you retain these honorable principles, there is little danger of your wanting opportunities to call them forth into action. The momentous enterprize in which your country is engaged is not to be accomplished in this, or that year. If, in no longer a period than the siege of Troy, we bring all our mighty schemes to bear, it will be the greatest work that ever was perfected in so little a time. You have set your heart, you tell me, on a military employment. This is the usual bent of young men; and, as it was my own, it will be with an ill grace, that I reprehend it in you. But, with the experience that I have had of it, I should be wanting in that love and esteem I owe you, should I hesitate to tell you that, as your father, there is not a profession you could have chosen in which I should not more cordially have concurred with you. Yet, I love arms; I am married to my sword, as well as to your most amiable mother: and herein is my witness, that I am in earnest when I say, death alone shall divorce me from either. I am not so blindly devoted, however,

however, to my profession, as not to see by how frail a tenure I hold the little reputation I have in it. As a statesman, as a senator, it is in the general, sufficient that you mean well, that you are careful to qualify yourself to form a right judgment of the true interests of your country, and that, with the honest impartiality of a free man, you have still exerted your best endeavors to promote those interests. But, with a soldier, success alone is merit; and there is nothing that can atone for the want of it. The world is a worse judge of military matters, than any other. It would astonish you to find, on a minute comparison, how very little difference there was in the skill and spirit which guided Braddock and Wolfe in the last actions of their lives. But, how different has been their fate!—I think, I am not without some talents for the line of life, which has fallen to my lot. But, opposed as I must be by men, probably, of infinitely superior skill, and encompassed moreover with such hosts of other difficulties and discouragements as I am, it is not mine to command success.* And, when

---

* The reader of Washington's letters cannot fail to notice how few are the references to matters of history, and how seldom there is any evidence of an acquaintance with even the writings generally understood at that time. A single instance, that I have met with, may here be cited. In a letter to Deputy Governor Cooke, 29 October, 1775, he wrote: "But it is not in our power to command success, though it is always our duty to deserve it," and in one to Colonel Benedict Arnold, 5 December, 1775, he said: "It is not in the power of any man to command success, but you have done more, you have deserved it." As is well known, the lines occur in Addison's Cato:—

either

either my contemporaries, or future historians, shall sit in judgment on my conduct, if, haply, ill-fortune should overtake me, seeing our miscarriages only, and having neither curiosity nor ability to investigate the thousand causes which led to them, am I not too well warranted in concluding, that they will be attributed to mis-management? Have I not then reason to wish that your choice had fallen on the quieter but not less important calling of a private gentleman; in which, as a senator, you might have given proof of your abilities, in a way, in which fortune would not have had so great a share? But, notwithstanding all this, and if after all, you be irrevocably determined to try your fortune in the field, and you can gain your mother's and your wife's consent, I here give it you under my hand, that you shall not want mine. Most certainly there cannot be a more honorable employment: and if, (which Heaven avert,) Fortune should declare against you, my consolation will be that, I can assure myself, you will deserve to be successful. I will, on the opening of the next campaign, procure you an appointment to the command of a

---

"'Tis not in mortals to command success,
But we'll do more, Sempronius, we'll deserve it."

In a letter written to Mrs. George William Fairfax from the camp at Raystown, on the Bouquet expedition against Duquesne, in September, 1758, Washington wrote: "I should think our time more agreeably spent, believe me, in playing a part in Cato, with the company you mention, and myself doubly happy in being the Juba to such a Marcia as you must make."

regiment,

regiment, either here, or in the southern wing. And, if my opinion may have any weight with you, you will, for many reasons, prefer the being stationed in some of the southern states. There is no fear of its being an inactive station. I have little expectation that this year will close with aught considerably decisive on either side: and, if our enemies be able to hold out another campaign, it is most likely, their policy will be, by means of their naval superiority, to carry on a kind of an incursive war, by making unexpected descents in different and distant places. Meanwhile, permit me to press you to persevere in your attention to military matters. The manual exercise, which you were so justly dilligent to learn, whilst I was with you, is but the A. B. C. of your profession.* Neither will you profit so much as you might reasonably expect, from the study of those authors, who have written professedly on the art of war. This is like the learning the game of Whist by reading Hoyle. I have been witness to the mischievous effects of it. A man, book-learned only, does very well in the still scenes of marchings and encampments. But when, in the various bustles

---

* "As to the manual exercise, the evolutions and manœuvers of a regiment, with other knowledge necessary to a soldier, you will acquire them from those authors who have treated upon these subjects, among whom Bland (the newest edition) stands foremost; also an Essay on the Art of War; Instructions for Officers, lately published at Philadelphia; the Partisan; Young, and others." *Washington to Col. Woodford*, 10 November, 1776.

of actual war, a cause arises, as must often be the case, not described in his books, he is utterly at a loss. I would not, however, have you to understand me as if I meant to discourage your reading these books at all; so far from it, I would have you read them very often, and make yourself acquainted with the subject, as much as you can in theory. My caution meant only to guard you against placing too much reliance on them. Their best commentators, next to your own experience, will be the historians of Greece and Rome; which it is your happiness to be able to read in the originals. But the main and most essential qualification is an high sense of honor, an elevation of sentiment and a certain dignified stile of behavior, that distinguishes, or should distinguish, a soldier from every other man. It is a shame indeed, if he who undertakes to command others, has not first learned to command himself: I will not endure anything mean or sordid either in your principles, or your manners; having determined, if it were left with me, to be as strict and rigorous in these particulars, as were the knights of old, when a candidate was to be invested with the orders of chivalry. I cannot dissociate the ideas between a soldier and a gentleman: and however common it may be to give that last appellation to persons of every station and every character, it yet conveys to me an idea of worths which I want words to express. I am

not

not solicitous to pay you compliments, even by implication; but, I may certainly be permitted to say, that if I had not known you to be a gentleman, you never should have had my consent to your becoming a soldier.

Your observations on this important contest are just and accurate, and discover a reach of thought, and a penetration beyond what I had expected of you. What you say on the subject of independency is perfectly judicious, and, no doubt, highly worthy of all our most serious consideration. Yet, I have a præsentiment, that it will take place, and speedily. Open and unreserved as my conduct toward you has ever been, I have no reluctance to confess to you, that the measure is diametrically opposite to my judgment: for I have not yet despaired of an honorable reconciliation;* and whilst I can enter-

* "With respect to myself, I have never entertained an idea of an accommodation, since I heard of the measures which were adopted in consequence of the Bunker's Hill fight. The King's speech has confirmed the sentiments I entertained upon the news of that affair; and, if every man was of my mind, the ministers of Great Britain should know, in a few words, upon what issue the cause should be put. I would not be deceived by artful declarations, nor specious pretences; nor would I be amused by unmeaning propositions; but in open undisguises, and manly terms proclaim our wrongs, and our resolution to be redressed. I would tell them, that we had borne much, that we had long and ardently sought for reconciliation upon honorable terms, that it had been denied us, that all our attempts after peace had proved abortive, and had been grossly misrepresented, that we had done everything which could be expected from the best subjects, that the spirit of freedom beat too high in us to submit to slavery, and that, if nothing else could satisfy a tyrant and his diabolical ministry, we are determined to shake off all connexions with a state so unjust and unnatural. This I would tell them, not under covert, but in words as clear as the sun in its meridian brightness." *Washington to Reed*, 10 February, 1776.

tain

tain but an hope of that, both interest and inclination lead me to prefer it to every thing else upon earth. Human affairs are oddly ordered: to obtain what you most wish for, you must often make use of means you the least approve of. As in bargaining, to obtain a fair and equal price, you must frequently ask more than you wish to take. I do not really wish for independence: I hope there are few who do: but, I have never heard the reasonings of those, who have proved that, if we did not declare for it, we should fail to obtain the constitutional subordination to which we are entitled, fairly refuted. I would not have you, therefore, hastily conclude that if, in this struggle, we fall short of everything we have claimed; we are worsted: perhaps the very worst thing that could befal us, is that we should gain all. I do assure you that, in my opinion, the next misfortune to that of being thrust from our just rank in the order of freemen, would be the giving us up, and leaving us to ourselves. But, this Great Britain will never do, voluntarily: for, if ever she does, whatever may become of us, from that moment, she may date the commencement of her own downfall.

I am exceedingly happy in the becoming moderation which you observe and endeavor to introduce towards the unhappy men whose political creed differ from ours. But for this blot in her scutcheon, thrown on her by too many of her rash and unworthy

worthy advocates, by a contrary conduct, this effort of America would have done her honor, even though she had failed. I am shocked at the Instances of intolerance I daily hear of, and have no power to prevent. But, like the other evils of war, it is a calamity that unavoidably grows out of such a convulsion; and one might as well hope to stem the fury of a torrent, as to give laws to an enraged people. It is, however, the duty of every true friend to liberty, by every gentle and conciliatory means in his power to restrain it. And, I am happy to find this sentiment daily becoming more general amongst us. All things considered, I cannot but think it not a little to our honor that things have not been carried to still a greater height in this way.

Remember me affectionately to Nelly; and tell her, that though I should be most happy to see her, I may not hope for that happiness speedily: as the din of arms, I imagine, would be but unpleasing entertainment to her; and I have little prospect of any leisure, at least, before we go into winter quarters. I hope Mr. Calvert, and all the family are well: I beg to be remembered to them. I will write to your mother in a few days. You are very good in leaving her alone as little as may be. Continue to write to me frequently, freely, and fully: the hearing of my dearest friends and family's welfare being the only true happiness I have

any

any chance to enjoy amidst the perpetual hurry in which I live.

I am, my dear Jack,
Your very affectionate Friend and Father,
GEO. WASHINGTON.

TO THE HON. LADY WASHINGTON, ETC.*

24 JUNE, 1776.

MY DEAREST LIFE AND LOVE,

You have hurt me, I know not how much, by the insinuation in your last, that my letters to you have lately been less frequent, because I have felt less concern for you. The suspicion is most unjust; —may I not add, it is most unkind? Have we lived, now almost a score of years, in the closest and dearest conjugal intimacy to so little purpose that, on an appearance only of inattention to you, and which you might have accounted for in a thousand ways more natural and more probable, you should pitch upon that single motive which alone is injurious to me? I have not, I own, wrote so often to you as I wished and as I ought. But think of my situation, and then ask your heart, if I be *without excuse*. We are not, my dearest, in circumstances the most favourable to our happiness:

---

*The courtesy shown by General Howe on a later occasion, is worthy of record. "The enclosed letter having been intercepted and brought to me, I am happy to return it, without the least attempt being made to discover any part of its contents." *Howe to Washington*, 11 November, 1776.

"I am to acknowledge the honor of your favor of the 11th, ultimo, and to thank you for the polite return of my letter to Mrs. Washington." *Washington to Howe*, 1 December, 1776.

but let us not, I beseech you, idly make them worse by indulging suspicions and apprehensions which minds in distress are but too apt give way to. I never was, as you have often told me, even in my better and more disengaged days, so attentive to the little punctilios of friendship, as, it may be, became me: but, my heart tells me, there never was a moment in my life, since I first knew you, in which it did not cleave and cling to you with the warmest affection: and it must cease to beat, ere it can cease to wish for your happiness, above any thing on earth.

I congratulate you most cordially on the fair prospect of recovery of your amiable daughter-in-law;* nor can I wonder, that this second loss of a little one should affect you. I fear the fatigues of the journey, and the perpetual agitations of a camp, were too much for her. They are, however, both young and healthy; so that there can be little doubt of their soon repairing the loss.†

And now will my dearest love permit me, a little more earnestly than I have ever yet done, to press you to consent to that so necessary, so safe and so easy, though so dreadful a thing—the being inoculated? It was always adviseable; but at this

---

* Nelly Calvert, second daughter of Benedict Calvert. The marriage took place on the 3d of February, 1774.

† The children of John Parke Custis were: Elizabeth Parke, born 1776; Eleanor Parke, 1779; and George Washington Parke, 1781.

juncture

juncture it seems to be almost absolutely necessary.* I am far from sure, that that restless madman, our quondam governor,† from the mere lust of doing mischief, will not soon betake himself to the carry-

---

* What inoculation meant in those days may be conjectured from the following report made by the Board of War to the Continental Congress, 20 February, 1777: "That the Assembly of the State of Maryland be requested to deliver to Dr. McKensie, so much medicines of the following Denominations as he shall want and they can spare, to enable him to inoculate the Continental troops in this town, in the following proportions for one hundred men:

        Six ounces Calomel.
        Two pounds Jallop.
        Three pounds Nitre.
            Elix^r. Vitriol.
        One pound Peruvian Bark.
        One pound Virginia Snake Root.

At the request of Congress Washington had come to Philadelphia, arriving there on the afternoon of Thursday, May 23d. It was then that Mrs. Washington had determined to be inoculated for the small pox. Hancock had invited both the General and Mrs. Washington to stay at his house in Arch Street. "As the house I live in is large and roomy, it will be entirely in your power to live in that manner you should wish. Mrs. Washington may be as retired as she pleases while under the inoculation, and Mrs. Hancock will esteem it an honor to have Mrs. Washington inoculated in her house." *Hancock to Washington*, 21 May, 1776. This invitation does not appear to have been accepted, and from a sentence in Hancock's letter we are led to suppose that they went to the house of a "Mr. Randolph," who lived on Chestnut street. Mrs. Washington had reached the city before the General, for on the 31st she was in the "thirteenth day, and she has very few postules." *Washington to his brother*, 31 May, 1776. The tradition is that Mrs. Washington returned to Mount Vernon, when the British fleet had sailed from Boston, and it was from that place that she came to Philadelphia to undergo inoculation. We may thus set the dates against the plausibility of the letter, as it is absurd to suppose that Washington would raise the question of inoculation a month after it had actually been tried, and tried successfully. On July 24th, Washington wrote to Custis:

"Mrs. Washington is now at Philadelphia, and has thoughts of returning to Virginia, as there is little or no prospect of her being with me any part of this summer."

† Lord Dunmore.

ing

ing on a prædatory war in our rivers. And as Potomack will certainly be thought most favorable for his purposes, as affording him scope to keep without the reach of annoyance, I have little reason to flatter myself that it would not be particularly pleasing to him, to vent his spite at my house. Let him; it would affect me only as it would affect you; and, for this reason, among others, I wish you out of his reach. Yet I think I would not have you quit your house, professedly, from an apprehension of a visit from him. An appearance of fearfulness and timidity, even in a woman of my family, might have a bad effect; but, I must be something more or less than man, not to wish you out of the way of a danger, which, to say the least, must be disagreeable to you, and could do good to no one. All this makes for your going to Philadelphia, a place of perfect security; and it would almost be worth while to be inoculated, if it were only for the fair pretence it furnishes you with of quitting Virginia, at a time when I could not but be exceedingly uneasy at your remaining in it. But I flatter myself, any further argument will be unnecessary, when I shall add, as I now do, that till you have had the smallpox, anxiously as else I should wish for it, I never can think of consenting to your passing the winter here in quarters with me.*

---

* The writer was drawing upon his memory, perhaps more than upon his

I would

I would have Lund Washington immediately remove all the unmarried and suspicious of the slaves, to the quarters in Frederick. The Harvesting must be got in by hirelings. Let him not keep any large stock of grain trod out, especially at the mill, or within the reach of water carriage; and in particular, let as little as may be, be left at Clifton's quarters. It will not be too late, even in the first week of July, to sow the additional supply of hemp and flax-seed, which Mr. Mifflin * has secured for me in Philadelphia; and which I hope will be with you before this letter. For obvious reasons, you will not sow it on the island, nor by the water side. But I hope you will have a good account of

---

imagination. When in October, 1775, Washington invited his wife to come to the camp at Cambridge, it is very probable that he may have urged her then to undergo inoculation, for the disease was then in the soldiery. Such an idea may have suggested the reference in the letter, and, also, to the same period belongs this suggestion of a "predatory war in our rivers," by Lord Dunmore. Lund had written to the General in the fall of 1775: "Many people have made a stir about Mrs. Washington's continuing at Mount Vernon, but I cannot think there is any danger. The thought I believe originated in Alexandria; from thence it got to Loudoun, and I am told the people of Loudoun talk of sending a guard to conduct her to Berkeley, with some of their principal men to persuade her to leave this place and accept their offer. Mr. John Augustine Washington wrote, pressing her to leave Mount Vernon. She does not believe herself in danger. Lord Dunmore will hardly himself venture up this river; nor do I believe he will send on that errand. Surely her old acquaintence, the attorney, who with his family is on board his ship, would prevent his doing any act of that kind. You may depend I will be watchful, and upon the least alarm persuade her to remove."

Mrs Washington soon after left Mount Vernon, to join the General at Cambridge, in company with Mrs. Gates, her son Parke Custis and his wife, and Warner Lewis. They arrived in camp December 11th.

*Spelled Mitflin in Bew.

your

your crop on the Ohio. If Bridgey * continues refractory and riotous, though I know you can ill spare him, let him by all means be sent off, as I hope Jack Custis's boy Joe already is, for his sauciness, at Cambridge.

My attention is this moment called off to the discovery, or pretended discovery, of a most wild and daring plot.† It is impossible, as yet, to develope the mystery in which it either is, or is supposed to be involved. Thus much only I can find out with certainty, that it will be a fine field for a war of lies on both sides. No doubt it will make a good deal of noise in the country; and there are who think it useful to have the minds of the people kept constantly on the fret by rumors of this sort. For my part, I who am said to be the object principally aimed at in it, find myself perfectly at my ease; and I have mentioned it to you only from an apprehension that, hearing it from others and not from me, you might imagine I was in the midst of danger that I knew not of.

The perpetual solicitude of your poor heart about me, is certainly highly flattering to me; yet I should be happy to be able to quiet your fears. Why do you complain of my reserve? Or, how

---

* Probably intended for Breechy. In February 1760 Washington noted in his diary-almanac: "Breechy was laid up this morning with pains in his breast and head, and attended with a fever."

† This refers to the so-called Hickey plot. See *Minutes of a Conspiracy against the Liberties of America.*

could

could you imagine that I distrusted either your prudence or your fidelity? I have the highest opinion of them both. But why should I teaze you with tedious details of schemes and views which are perpetually varying; and which therefore might, not improbably mislead, where I meant to inform you? Suffice it that I say, what I have often before told you, that, as far as I have the controul of them, all our preparations of war, aim only at peace. Neither do I, at this moment, see the least likelihood of their being any considerable military operations this season; and, if not in this season, certainly in no other. It is impossible to suppose that, in the leisure, and quiet of winter quarters, men will not have the virtue to listen to the dictates of plain common sense and sober reason. The only true interest of both sides is reconciliation; nor can there be a point in the world clearer, than that both sides must be losers by war, in a manner which even peace will not soon compensate for. We must, at last, agree, and be friends; for we cannot live without them, and they will not without us: and a bystander might well be puzzled to find out, why as good terms cannot be given and taken now, as when we shall have well nigh ruined each other by the mutual madness of cutting one another's throats. For all these reasons, which cannot but be as obvious to the English commissioners, and ours, as they are to me,

me, I am at a loss to imagine how any thing can arise to obstruct a negotiation, and, of consequence, a pacification. You, who know my heart, know that there is not a wish nearer to it than this is; but I am prepared for every event, one only excepted—I mean a dishonourable peace. Rather than that, let me, though it be with the loss of every thing else I hold dear, continue this horrid trade, and, by the most unlikely means, be the unworthy instrument of preserving political security and happiness to them, as well as to ourselves. —Pity this cannot be accomplished, without fixing on me that sad name, Rebel. I love my King; you know I do: a soldier, a good man cannot but love him. How peculiarly hard then is our fortune to be deemed traitors to so good a King! But, I am not without hopes, that even he will yet see cause to do me justice: posterity, I am sure, will. Mean while, I comfort myself with the reflection that this has been the fate of the best and bravest men, even of the Barons who obtained Magna Charta, whilst the dispute was pending. This, however, anxiously as I wish for it, it is not mine to command: I see my duty, that of standing up for the liberties of my country; and whatever difficulties and discouragements lie in my way, I dare not shrink from it; and I rely on that Being, who has not left to us the choice of duties, that, whilst I conscientiously discharge mine, I shall not finally
lose

lose my reward. If I really am not a bad man, I shall not long be so set down.*

Assure yourself, I will pay all possible attention to your recommendations. But happy as I am in an opportunity of obliging you, even in the smallest things, take it not amiss, that I use the freedom with you to whisper in your ear, to be sparing of them. You know how I am circumstanced: hardly the promotion of a subaltern is left to me.† And, free and independent as I am, I resolve to remain so. I owe the Congress no obligations for any personal favours done to myself; nor will I run in debt to them for favours to others. Besides, I am mortified to have to ask of them, what, in sound policy (if other motives had been wanting) they ought to have granted to me, unasked. I cannot describe to you the inconveniences this army suffers for want of this consequence being given to its

---

*" The reflection on my situation, and that of the army, produces many an uneasy hour when all around me are wrapped in sleep. Few people know the predicament we are in, on a thousand accounts; fewer still will believe, if any disaster happens to these lines, from what causes it flows. I have often thought how much happier I should have been, if, instead of accepting of a command under such circumstances, I had taken my musket on my shoulder and entered the ranks, or, if I could have justified the measure to posterity and my own conscience, had retired to the back country, and lived in a wigwam. If I shall be able to rise superior to these and many other difficulties, which might be enumerated, I shall most religiously bebelieve that the finger of Providence is in it, to blind the eyes of our enemies." *Washington to Joseph Reed,* 14 January, 1776.

†" I have no friend whom I want to bring in, nor any person with whom I am in the least connected, that I wish to promote." *Washington to the Council of Massachusetts Bay,* 10 January, 1776.

commander

commander in chief. But, as these might be increased, were my peculiar situation in this respect generally known, I forbear; only enjoining you a cautious silence on this head.—In a regular army, our Virginia young men, would certainly, in general, make the best officers; but I regret that they have not now put it in my power justly to pay them this compliment. They dislike their northern allies; and this dislike is the source of infinite mischiefs and vexations to me. In the many disputes and quarrels of this sort which we have had, one thing has particularly struck me. My countrymen are not inferior in understanding; and are certainly superior in that distinguished spirit and high sense of honour which should form the character of an officer. Yet, somehow or other, it for ever happens, that in every altercation, they are proved to be in the wrong; and they expect of me attentions and partialities which it is not in my power to shew them.

Let me rely that your answer to this will be dated in Philadelphia. If I am not very busily engaged, (which, I hope may not be the case,) perhaps I may find ways and means to pay you a visit of a day or two; but this I rather hint as what I wish, than what I dare bid you expect. If you still think the fragments of the set of greys I bought of Lord Bottetourt unequal to the journey, let Lund Washington sell them, singly, or otherwise

wise as he can to the best advantage, and purchase a new set of bays. I could, as you desire, get them here, and perhaps on better terms; but, I have a notion, whether well or ill founded I know not, that they never answer well in Virginia. I beg to be affectionately remembered to all our friends and relations; and that you will continue to believe me to be

Your most faithful and tender Husband.

G. W.*

---

* "The letter said to be the General's, is partly genuine and partly spurious. Those who metamorphosed the intercepted original committed an error in point of time, for Mrs. Washington was with the General in New York at the date of it." *John Laurens to his father,* 23 January, 1778.

Laurens was at this time a member of the General's family.

TO MR. LUND WASHINGTON, AT MOUNT VERNON, FAIRFAX COUNTY, VIRGINIA.

NEW YORK, July the 16th, 1776.

DEAR LUND,

We are still going on with all imaginable briskness and success with our works, which, I think are already impregnable. It would really astonish you to see the progress we have made. I do not believe that all history can furnish a precedent of so much being done in so little a time, or, in so masterly a manner, where you had so little right to look for consummate skill.* If in every thing else, we could but come up to our exertions in these fortifications, I should hardly know how to doubt the judgment of those who think that we may bid defiance to the world. But, I know not how it is, I am diffident of every thing. Whilst almost every body else seem to have persuaded themselves

---

* "I believe I may with great truth affirm, that no man perhaps since the first institution of armies, ever commanded one under more difficult circumstances." *Washington to his brother*, 31 March, 1776.

"It is not in the pages of history, perhaps, to furnish a case like ours. To maintain a post within musket shot of the enemy, for six months together, without [powder] and at the same time to disband one army, and recruit another, within that distance of twenty-odd British regiments, is more, probably, than ever was attempted." *Washington to the President of Congress*, 4 January, 1776.

themselves that we have nothing to fear, I alone torment myself with thinking that everything is against us. Even from these very works which have inspired us with such confidence, I anticipate only misfortune and disgrace. By this time the die is cast, and America is authoritatively declared free and independent. And, unless we can be contented to appear ridiculous in the eyes of all the world, we must resolve to support this declaration by a suitable conduct ;—we must fight our way to freedom and independency; for, in no other way, shall we be permitted to obtain it, farther than in words.*

A war, therefore, and a most serious one, is now inevitable. Next to good finances, which it is not my province to provide for, a good army is, doubtless, a main requisite to the carrying on of a successful war. And a good army is, by no means,

---

* The Declaration reached Washington on the 9th, and was announced in the *General Orders* of that date.

"I perceive that Congress have been employed in deliberating on measures of the most interesting nature. It is certain, that it is not with us to determine in many instances what consequences will flow from our counsels ; but yet it behoves us to adopt such, as, under the smiles of a gracious and all-kind Providence, will be most likely to promote our happiness. I trust the late decisive part they have taken is calculated for that end, and will secure us that freedom and those privileges, which have been and are refused us, contrary to the voice of nature and the British constitution. Agreeably to the request of Congress, I caused the *Declaration* to be proclaimed before all the army under my immediate command ; and have the pleasure to inform them that the measure seemed to have their most hearty assent ; the expressions and behaviour, both of officers and men, testifying their warmest approbation of it." *To the President of Congress*, 10 July, 1776.

secured

secured, as some seem to reckon, by securing a large number of men. We want soldiers; and between these, and raw, undisciplined men, there is a wide difference.* The question then is, how are these raw and undisciplined men to be formed into good soldiers? And I am free to give it as my opinion, that so far from contributing to this, will strong holds, fortified posts, and deep intrenchments be found, that they will have a direct contrary effect. To be a soldier is to be inured to, and familiar with danger; to dare to look your enemy in the face, unsheltered and exposed to their fire, and even when repulsed, to rally again with undiminished spirit. The Indian maxim is, that it is equally your duty to take care of yourself and to annoy your enemy. To a general, this may not be an unusual caution; but I will venture to assert, that whenever a private sentinel allows himself to act on this principle, the odds are, that, in the moment of trial, in his exceeding solicitude not to forget the former, the latter will be but little attended to. Now, what I ask, are all these mighty ditches and breast-works, but so many lessons and admonitions to our men of what prodigious

---

* In a letter to Reed (10 February, 1776), Washington used the words "raw and undisciplined troops." Hancock spoke of an "undisciplined band of husbandmen," which under Washington's rule, had "in the course of a few months become soldiers." "They were indeed," Washington feelingly echoed, "a band of undisciplined husbandmen." *Washington to the President of Congress*, 18 April, 1776.

importance

importance it is to take care of themselves? It would be almost worth our while to be defeated, if it were only to train us to stand fire, and to bear a reverse of fortune with a decent magnanimity. If it had not been for this ill-judged humour of fighting from behind a screen, the 19th of April,* the 17th of June† last year, might have been the happiest days America ever saw. All these things have I, again and again, represented to my masters; I am ashamed to say, to how little purpose. They return me answers and instructions, which, though I cannot refute, have not yet convinced what I would call the feelings of my own mind.‡

* Lexington.
† Bunker's Hill.
‡ "I think then we might have attacked 'em long before this and with success, were our troops differently constituted; but the fatal persuasion has taken deep root in the minds of the Americans from the highest to the lowest order, that they are no match for the Regulars, but when covered by a wall or breastwork. This notion is still further strengthened by the endless works we are throwing up. In short, unless we can remove the idea (and it must be done by degrees), no spirited action can be ventured on without the greatest risk." *Major General Charles Lee to Benjamin Rush*, 19 September, 1775.

"The account given of the behaviour of the men under General Montgomery, is exactly consonant to the opinion I have formed of these people. Place them behind a parapet, a breastwork, stone wall, or anything that will afford them shelter, and from their knowledge of a firelock they will give a good account of their enemy; but I am as well convinced, as if I had seen it, that they will not march boldly up to a work, nor stand exposed in a plain; and yet, if we are furnished with the means, and the weather will afford us a passage, and we can get in men, for these three things are necessary, something must be attempted. The men must be brought to face danger; they cannot always have an intrenchment or a stone wall as a safeguard or shield." *Washington to Joseph Reed*, 1 February, 1776.

"To be plain, these people—among friends—are not to be depended

This

This day week,* the enemy's fleet was first descried off Sandy Hook. They have been employed since then, in debarking their troops on Staten Island, where they are cantoned, as far as I can judge, in a very uncompact and unguarded manner; I cannot exactly ascertain their number, but I have reason to believe, that they fall short of 7000.† It is more extraordinary still, that I am not able to inform you of the exact number of forces under my own command.‡ I fancy, however, we might bring into the field, at this place, double their number at a minute's warning; and with this superiority of numbers, making all possible allowances for our other disadvantages, one would hope we might be able to give a good account of them. You, who are sanguine in the extreme, and all impatience, will eagerly ask, why we suffered them to land unmolested, and to remain so ever since. What excellent expeditions your fire side generals can instantly plan and execute!§

---

upon if exposed; and any man will fight well if he thinks himself in no danger. I do not apply this only to these people. I suppose it to be the case with all raw and undisciplined troops. *Washington to Joseph Reed*, 10 February, 1776.

* Monday, July 1.

† He learned from four prisoners, who were taken on the 7th, that Howe had about ten thousand men.

‡ On July 13 the returns showed 14,669 rank and file, of whom 10,319 were fit for duty.

§ "I observe what you say in respect to the ardor of the chimney corner heroes," *Washington to Reed*, 10 February, 1776.

But

But you forget that they are posted on an island, and that we have no way of coming at them unless they would lend us their ships and boats, which I have not presumed to ask of them. Aware, however, of the importance of falling on them, whilst there is a chance of doing it with success, and e'er they become a match for us, by reinforcements, which they daily expect, I have formed a scheme, which at least, is plausible, and promises fair to be successful. I have submitted it to Congress; and every moment expect their answer; and if they will but support me with alacrity, and in good earnest, my next, I trust, will not be quite so desponding. I expect to be all ready to put my plan in execution on Tuesday, or, at farthest, on Wednesday night: so that, probably, at the very moment you are reading this, we may be engaged in a very different service. You will, no doubt, be impatient to hear from me as soon as may be after Wednesday; and I will not disappoint you. Meanwhile, I shall not need to tell you, that end how it will, all that I freely chatter to you, is to remain a profound secret to everybody else.*

---

* So far from meditating acting on the offensive, Washington was deploring the weakness of his army, calling in militia and the Continental regiments from the Eastward to his aid, urging the formation of the Flying Camp, and even looking to the Indians of St. John's, Nova Scotia, and Penobscot for assistance. On the 11th he congratulated himself that they had yet made no attack, waiting, as some deserters said, for the arrival of Lord Howe. "We are strengthening ourselves as much as possible, and deem their staying out so long a fortunate circumstance, as it not only

Doctor, now Brigadier-general Mercer, is here, and is a great comfort to me.* Like myself, he wants experience; but he is very shrewd and sensible, and though a Scotchman, is remarkably humane and liberal. I have communicated the whole of my designs to him alone; and I am not ashamed to own that I have received much assistance from him. I know not how it may turn out; but though neither he nor I are very apt to be sanguine, we have both confessed to be so on this occasion. Animated, however, as I feel myself with the near prospect of at length doing something, not unworthy the high rank to which I am raised, I own to you I take a serious pleasure in it, only as it flatters me with the hope of thereby obtaining a speedier and happier peace. Let us, since war must be our lot, distinguish ourselves as freemen should, in fields of blood: still remembering, however, that we fight not for conquest, but for liberty.

I am with the truest esteem, Dear Lund, your faithful Friend and Servant. G. W.

---

gives us an opportunity of advancing our works, but of getting some relief from the neighboring provinces." *Washington to Major General Schuyler*, 11 July, 1776. Not until the 12th was the proposition of making a general attack on the enemy's quarters on the island submitted to the general officers and judged to be inadvisable.

* Mercer arrived in camp on Tuesday, July 2d, and the next morning was ordered into New Jersey to prevent, if possible, the enemy's crossing from Staten Island.

TO MR. LUND WASHINGTON, &C.

NEW YORK, JULY 8, 1777.*

DEAR LUND,

How cruelly are all my hopes in one sad moment, blasted and destroyed! I am positively ordered to wait for the enemy in our lines;† and lest I should be mad enough not to obey their mandates, not a single tittle of anything I had asked for, is granted. Thus has a second opportunity of rendering my country an essential service, in the way of my profession, been unwisely and in the most mortifying manner denied me. I profess, I hardly know how to bear it: having to regret not only, that two opportunities, such as may never again occur, have been suffered to pass by us unimproved: but that none can happen, we

---

* An evident misprint.

† "You have had many rumors propagated among you which I suppose you know not how to account for. One was that Congress, the last summer, had tied the hands of General Washington, and would not let him fight, particularly on the White Plains. This report was totally groundless." *John Adams to his wife,* 6 April, 1777.

Congress on September 3d, directed Washington to take "especial care" in case he should find it necessary to quit New York, that "no damage be done to New York," which was interpreted by some to mean that the city was to be maintained at every hazard. Congress was obliged to explain that such was not its intention. *Journals of Congress,* September 3d and 10th; *Washington to the President of Congress,* September 2d, 6th, 14th.

can improve. Managed as matters are, we neither are, nor ever shall be, a military people: and yet, in the train in which things are now put, unless we are, it were idiotism to hope for either freedom or independence.

I remember well, in a conversation I once had with a friend, now, most unjustly as well as unwisely, driven from his friends and his home, on the subject of monarchies and republics, he objected to the unavoidable slowness and dilatoriness of the executive power in the latter. Aiming to answer him in his own way, I replied that, if popular councils were slow, they yet were sure, and that *in the multitude of counsellors there is safety*. His answer was prophetical. If ever (he said) we of these countries should rashly put these things to the proof, it would be found, that, however true this adage might be in the cabinet, it was not so in the field. Convinced, by melancholy experience, that this is the case, and that, without some different system, we shall but expose ourselves to contempt and ruin, I resolve this evening honestly and openly to say so to the Congress.* I will go farther, and add, that if they

---

* " An army formed of good officers moves like clockwork; but there is no situation upon earth less enviable, nor more distressing, than that person's who is at the head of troops which are regardless of order and discipline, and who are unprovided with almost every necessary. In a word, the difficulties, which have forever surrounded me since I have been in the service, and kept my mind constantly upon the stretch, the wounds, which my feelings as an officer have received by a thousand things, which have happened, cannot,

cannot, in fact, as well as in appearance, trust me with the uncontrolled command of their army, I will no longer be their puppet. Why should I;— it being now morally certain that by going on as

pened contrary to my expectation and wishes; the effect of my own conduct, and present appearance of things, so little pleasing to myself, as to render it a matter of no surprise to me if I should stand capitally censured by Congress; added to a consciousness of my inability to govern an army composed of such discordant parts, and under such a variety of intricate and perplexing circumstances;—induces not only a belief, but a thorough conviction in my mind, that it will be impossible, unless there is a thorough change in our military system, for me to conduct matters in such a manner as to give satisfaction to the public, which is all the recompense I aim at, or ever wished for." *Washington to the President of Congress*, 24 September, 1776.

"The amazement which you seem to be in at the unaccountable measures which have been adopted by [Congress] would be a good deal increased if I had time to unfold the whole system of their management since this time twelve months. I do not know how to account for the unfortunate steps which have been taken but from that fatal idea of conciliation which prevailed so long—fatal, I call it, because from my soul I wish it may not prove so, though my fears lead me to think there is too much danger of it. This time last year I pointed out the evil consequences of short enlistments, the expenses of militia, and the little dependence that was to be placed in them. I assured [Congress] that the longer they delayed raising a standing army, the more difficult and chargeable would they find it to get one, and that, at the same time that the militia would answer no valuable purpose, the frequent calling them in would be attended with an expense, that they could have no conception of. Whether, as I have said before, the unfortunate hope of reconciliation was the cause, or the fear of a standing army prevailed, I will not undertake to say; but the policy was to engage men for twelve months only. The consequence of which, you have had great bodies of militia in pay that never were in camp; you have had immense quantities of provisions drawn by men that never rendered you one hour's service (at least usefully), and this is the most profuse and wasteful way. Your stores have been expended, and every kind of military [discipline?] destroyed by them; your numbers fluctuating, uncertain, and forever far short of report—at no one time, I believe, equal to twenty thousand men fit for duty. At present our number fit for duty (by this day's report) amount to 14,759, besides 3,427 on command, and the enemy within stone's throw of us. It is true a body of militia are again ordered out, but they come without any conveniences and soon return. I discharged a regiment the other

we

we have hitherto done, I can neither bring honor nor profit to them ; and yet am sure to lose all the little of either which I either have, or might have, possessed.*

day that had in it fourteen rank and file fit for duty only, and several that had less than fifty. In short, such is my situation that if I were to wish the bitterest curse to an enemy on this side of the grave, I should put him in my stead with my feelings ; and yet I do not know what plan of conduct to pursue. I see the impossibility of serving with reputation, or doing any essential service to the cause by continuing in command, and yet I am told that if I quit the command inevitable ruin will follow from the distraction that will ensue. In confidence I tell you that I never was in such an unhappy, divided state since I was born. To lose all comfort and happiness on the one hand, whilst I am fully persuaded that under such a system of management as has been adopted, I cannot have the least chance for reputation, nor those allowances made which the nature of the case requires ; and to be told, on the other, that if I leave the service all will be lost, is at the same time that I am bereft of every peaceful moment, distressing to a degree. But I will be done with the subject, with the precaution to you that it is not a fit one to be publicly known or discussed. If I fail, it may not be amiss that these circumstances be known, and declaration made in credit to the justice of my character. And if the men will stand by me (which by the by I despair of), I am resolved not to be forced from this ground while I have life; and a few days will determine the point, if the enemy should not change their plan of operations ; for they certainly will not—I am sure they ought not—to waste the season that is now fast advancing, and must be precious to them. I thought to have given you a more explicit account of my situation, expectation, and feelings, but I have not time. I am wearied to death all day with a variety of perplexing circumstances—disturbed at the conduct of the militia, whose behaviour and want of discipline has done great injury to the other troops, who never had officers, except in a few instances, worth the bread they eat. My time, in short, is so much engrossed that I have not leisure for corresponding, unless it is on mere matters of public business." *Washington to Lund Washington*, 30 September, 1776.

* "I am not fond of stretching my powers, and if the Congress will say, ' Thus far and no farther you shall go,' I will promise not to offend whilst I continue in their service." *Washington to Joseph Reed*, 3 March, 1776. Washington was named dictator in December, 1776.

Washington's policy about this time was outlined in a letter to the President of Congress, dated September 8th, 1776 :—

" Before the landing of the enemy in Long Island, the point of attack

I want

I want words to express to you what I have felt, and still do fell (*sic*) on this disappointment of all my hopes: I had allowed myself to build too much on my scheme; and I seem to be in the situation

could not be known, nor any satisfactory judgment formed of their intentions. It might be on Long Island, on Bergen, or directly on the city. This made it necessary to be prepared for each, and has occasioned an expense of labor, which now seems useless, and is regretted by those, who form a judgment from after-knowledge. But I trust, that men of discernment will think differently, and see that by such works and preparations we have not only delayed the operations of the campaign, till it is too late to effect any capital incursion into the country, but have drawn the enemy's forces to one point, and obliged them to decline their plan, so as to enable us to form our defence on some certainty.

"In deliberating on this great question, it was impossible to forget, that history, our own experience, the advice of our ablest friends in Europe, the fears of the enemy, and even the declarations of Congress, demonstrate, that on our side the war should be defensive (it has ever been called a war of posts), that we should on all occasions avoid a general action, nor put anything to risk, unless compelled by a necessity into which we ought never to be drawn.

"The arguments on which such a system was founded were deemed unanswerable; and experience has given her sanction. With these views, and being fully persuaded, that it would be presumption to draw out our young troops into open ground against their superiors both in number and discipline, I have never spared the spade and pickaxe. I confess I have not found that readiness to defend even strong posts at all hazards, which is necessary to derive the greatest benefits from them. The honor of making a brave defence does not seem to be a sufficient stimulus, when success is very doubtful, and the falling into the enemy's hands probable; but, I doubt not, this will be gradually attained. We are now in a strong post, but not an impregnable one, nay, acknowledged by every man of judgment to be untenable, unless the enemy will make the attack upon lines, when they can avoid it, and their movements indicate that they mean to do so.

"To draw the whole army together in order to arrange the defence proportionate to the extent of lines and works, would leave the country open for an approach, and put the fate of this army and its stores on the hazard of making a successful defence in the city, or the issue of an engagement out of it. On the other hand, to abandon a city, which has been by some deemed defensible, and on whose works much labor has been bestowed,

of

of one who should be allowed to rise, on purpose only to be thrown down. The enemy, in the midst of all our blusterings, must despise us; and, did not shame or some better principle restrain them, I should be but little surprised to find General Howe, even with his present little handful, attacking us,—yes, attacking us in our entrenchments. What shall I do? to retreat is to entail on myself the curses of every public man in my country; and to go on is certain ruin and disgrace. Were the world to know only my true history on this trying occasion, I persuade myself, all the candid and considerate in it would acquit me of

---

has a tendency to dispirit the troops, and enfeeble our cause. It has also been considered as the key to the northern country. But as to that, I am fully of opinion, that by the establishing of strong posts at Mount Washington on the upper part of this island, and on the Jersey side opposite to it, with the assistance of the obstructions already made, and which may be improved, in the water, that not only the navigation of Hudson's River, but an easier and better communication may be more effectually secured between the northern and southern states. . .

"I am sensible a retreating army is encircled with difficulties; that declining an engagement subjects a general to reproach; and that the common cause may be affected by the discouragement it may throw over the minds of many. Nor am I insensible of the contrary effects, if a brilliant stroke could be made with any probability of success, especially after our loss upon Long Island. But, when the fate of America may be at stake on the issue, when the wisdom of cooler moments and experienced men have decided, that we should protract the war if possible, I cannot think it safe or wise to adopt a different system, when the season for action draws so near to a close. That the enemy mean to winter in New York, there can be no doubt; that, with such an armament, they can drive us out. is equally clear. The Congress having resolved, that it should not be destroyed, nothing seems to remain, but to determine the time of their taking possession. It is our interest and wish to prolong it as much as possible, provided the delay does not affect our future measures."

blame.

blame. But this the world can know only by my resolving to tell a tale which, considering the rank I now hold in it, must involve my country in such internal broils and quarrels, as must be fatal to the glorious cause in which we have embarked. And this, I trust, I shall have the virtue never to do, be my private wrongs and sufferings ever so great.

I have finished my letter to the Congress, to whom I have, at length, spoken in a more peremptory tone, than, I fancy, they have been used to. It was absolutely necessary; and I should ill deserve their confidence if, through any mistaken complaisance or diffidence, I hesitated to point out to them the mischievous consequences of their interference. I have also insisted on precise instructions in what manner I am to conduct myself towards the British commissioners, if peradventure, as is possible, their first overtures should be made through me. Their answer will have a great influence on all my future measures; as I shall then know, (and surely it is time I should) on what ground I stand.* The very decided and adventur-

---

* Congress had been singularly remiss in this matter. Early in March rumors of the powers and objects of the commission of reconciliation given to Howe had reached the camp at Cambridge (*Washington to Reed*, 7 March, 1776), and on the 24th, Washington asked Congress for instructions on the reception of the Commissioners. "If they come to Boston, which probably will be the case if they come to America at all, I shall be under much embarrassment respecting the manner of receiving them, and the mode of treatment that ought to be used. I therefore pray that Congress will give me directions, and point out the line of conduct to be pursued; whether they are to be considered as ambassadors, and to have a pass or permit for

ous measure, which Congress itself has just taken, is big with the most important consequences, not only to the community at large, but to every man in it. The temper and judgment which they shall now manifest, on their first avowed assumption of the reins of government, will be indicative of what we may hereafter expect. Hoping for the best, I yet will watch them most carefully.

repairing through the country to Philadelphia, or to any other place; or whether they are to be restrained in any and what manner. I shall anxiously wait their orders, and whatever they are, comply with them literally."

This question offered no little difficulty to Congress, constituted as it then was, and containing a number of active minds ready to seize upon an opportunity of ending the contest by a reconciliation with the mother country. It was not until May 6th that the following resolution was adopted: "*Resolved*, That General Washington be informed, that Congress suppose, if the Commissioners are intended to be sent from Great Britain to treat for peace, that the usual practice in such cases will be observed, by making previous application for the necessary passports or safe conduct; and on such application being made, Congress will then direct the proper measures for the reception of such Commissioners." This is a singular resolution, for it provides for only one contingency, and that a somewhat remote one; that is, if the Commissioners come to treat for peace, and should apply for passports. Suppose they did not come to treat for peace, or should not apply for passports? Yet meagre as was the resolve, it was regarded as a triumph for the party in Congress who favored independence. "It will be observed," noted John Adams on this resolution, "how long this trifling business had been depending, but it cannot be known from the journal how much debate it had occasioned. It was one of those delusive contrivances by which the party in opposition to us endeavored, by lulling the people with idle hopes of reconciliation into security, to turn their heads and thoughts from independence. They endeavored to insert in the resolution ideas of reconciliation. We carried our point for inserting peace. They wanted powers to be given to the General to receive the Commissioners in ceremony; we ordered nothing to be done till we were solicited for passports. Upon the whole, we avoided the snare, and brought the controversy to a close with some dignity. But it will never be known how much labor it cost us to accomplish it." *Works*, III, 43.

The framing of the Declaration of Independence did more to check the efforts of the Commissioners than any other one circumstance.

'Tis

'Tis all fearful expectation: every man I see seems to be employed in preparing himself for the momentous rencontre, which every man persuades himself must shortly come on. There is an ostensible eagerness and impetuosity amongst us, I could willingly have excused: I should have been better pleased with that steady composure which distinguishes veterans. One thing is in our favour: the passions of our soldiery are seldom suffered to subside; being constantly agitated by some strange rumour or other. Happen what will, it can hardly be more extraordinary, than some one or other is perpetually presaging. And we have already performed such feats of valour, whilst we have no enemies to engage but such as our own imaginations manufacture for us, that I cannot but hope we shall do well, merely because no one seems to entertain a suspicion that we shall not. I can, as yet, give no guess, where or when they will approach us: I conclude, however, that they will hardly stir, till they are joined by all the men they expect. Desponding as I am, I wish they were arrived; and that, at this moment, they were in a condition to attack us: they may gain by procrastination, but we are sure to lose.*

I wrote to Mrs. Washington lately, and shall again in a week or two, if I do not hear from her

---

* It was not until August 18th that Washington could inform Congress that all the British force had arrived.

ere

ere that in Philadelphia. It has surprised me, that after what I wrote, she should hesitate. I beg of you, if she be still fearful, to second my persuasions by every means in your power. Exposed as she must be to so many interviews with people in the army, all of whom are in the way of the small-pox, I have the most dreadful apprehensions on her account. I know not well how the notion came into my head, but it is certain, I have, for several days, persuaded myself that she is already inoculated; and that out of tenderness and delicacy, she forbears to inform me of it, till she can also inform me she is out of danger.*

I note sundry particulars in your letter, to which I am not solicitous to give you answers. Why, when you have so often asked me in vain, will you press me for Congress-secrets? Whatever your or my private sentiments or wishes may be, it is sufficient for us that we know the highest authority in our country has declared it free and independent. All that is left for us to do is, so far as we can, to support this declaration, without too curiously enquiring into either its wisdom or its justice. I firmly believe, that the advocates for

---

* Washington had resorted to this deceit in 1770 when Jacky Custis went up to Baltimore to be inoculated. "I have withheld from her [Mrs. W.] the information you gave me in respect to his undertaking, and purpose, if possible, to keep her in total ignorance of his having been there, till I hear of his return, or perfect recovery." *Washington to Dr. Boucher*, 20 April, 1770.

this

this measure, meant well; and I pay them but an ordinary compliment in thinking that they were fitter to determine on a point of this sort, than either you or I are. At any rate, the world must allow it to be a spirited measure; and all I have to wish for is, that we may support it with a suitable spirit.

    I am, my Dear Lund,
      Yours most affectionately,
         G. W.

TO MR. LUND WASHINGTON, &C.

NEW YORK, July 15, 1776.

DEAR LUND,

Last Friday, the British fleet was seen off Staten-Island: they have since been employed, uninterrupted by us, in debarking their men, stores, &c.* And as they must now, I should imagine, be pretty nearly as strong as they expect to be this campaign, no doubt we shall soon hear of their motions. I have reason to believe, their first essay will not be on this, but on Long-Island; where (injudiciously I think,) we also are, or soon shall be in force. † Yet, if we do but act our parts as

---

*The first intimation that Washington received of the approach of the British fleet from Halifax was contained in a letter from Lieutenant Davison of the armed sloop *Schuyler*, that reached him on the 28th of June. For a day or two, three or four ships would drop in, and on the 29th, forty-five came in sight, confirming Davison's report, and before evening one hundred and ten had been counted. The story was that Howe had sailed from Halifax with 132 vessels, so nearly all the fleet arrived by the 31st. On the 2nd of July, 50 of them came into the Bay and anchored on the Staten Island side; the landing was made on the 9th. The "last Friday" mentioned in the letter, would have been the 12th. The last division of the fleet, bearing the Hessian auxiliaries, did not enter the harbor until the 12th of August.

† "I had determined to disembark the army at Gravesend bay in Long Island, and with this intention the fleet moved up the bay on the 1st. instant in the evening, in order to land the troops at the break of day next morning; but being more particularly informed during the night of a

become

become us, be the issue as it may, we shall at least give them no pleasing earnest of what they have to expect in the course of the war. But there is no relying on any plan that is to be executed by raw men. *

You have heard much of the powers with which commissioners were to be invested, for the purpose of settling the dispute. Like most other things belonging to it, these too have made a much greater figure in talk, than they do in fact. There are but two commissioners, the two Howes; and their powers are extremely vague and undefined.†

---

strong post upon a ridge of craggy heights covered with woods that lay in the route the army must have taken, only two miles distant from the enemy's works, and seven from Gravesend . . . I declined the undertaking." *General Howe to Lord George Germaine*, 7 July, 1776.

* Many illustrative sentences could be selected from his letters on this point. I give only one selection, occurring in his letter of September 24th, 1776, to the President of Congress :—

"The jealousy of a standing army, and the evils to be apprehended from one, are remote, and, in my judgment, situated and circumstanced as we are, not at all to be dreaded ; but the consequence of wanting one, according to my ideas formed from the present view of things, is certain and inevitable ruin. For, if I was called upon to declare upon oath, whether the militia have been most serviceable or hurtful upon the whole, I should subscribe to the latter. I do not mean by this, however, to arraign the conduct of Congress ; in so doing I should equally condemn my own measures, if I did not my judgment; but experience, which is the best criterion to work by, so fully, clearly, and decisively reprobates the practice of trusting to militia, that no man, who regards order, regularity, and economy, or who has any regard for his own honor, character, or peace of mind, will risk them upon this issue."

† " It is a great stake we are playing for, and sure we are of winning, if the cards are well managed. Inactivity in some, disaffection in others, and timidity in many, may hurt the cause. Nothing else can ; for unanimity will carry us through triumphantly, in spite of every exertion of Great Britain, if we are linked together in one indissoluble bond. This the

It

It is a pity, methinks, that Congress had not had better information on this subject: if they had, it is to be presumed, they would not have precipitated the declaration for independency, so as to preclude all possibility of negotiation. I may venture to whisper it in your ear, that this excepted, I firmly believe, that America might have carried every other point: and, certainly, there was a time, when this would have been deemed a conquest beyond the warmest wishes of the warmest American. Whether in the present posture of affairs, it still be so, is another question: I can answer only

---

leaders know, and they are practising every stratagem to divide us, and unite their own people. Upon this principle it is, that the restraining bill is passed, and commissioners are coming over. The device, to be sure, is shallow, the covering thin, but they will hold out to their own people, that the acts complained of are repealed, and commissioners sent to each colony to treat with us, and that we will attend to neither of them. This upon weak minds among us, will have its effect. They wish for reconciliation: or, in other words, they wish for peace without attending to the conditions." *Washington to his brother*, 31 March, 1776.

"When the letter and declaration, from Lord Howe, to Mr. Franklin and the other late governors, come to be published, I should suppose the warmest advocates for dependence on the British crown must be silent, and be convinced beyond all possibility of doubt, that all that has been said about the Commissioners was illusory, and calculated expressly to deceive and put off their guard, not only the good people of our own country, but those of the English nation, that were averse to the proceedings of the King and ministry. Hence we see the cause why a specification of their powers was not given to the mayor and city of London, on their address, requesting it. That would have been dangerous, because it would then [have] been manifest, that the line of conduct they were to pursue would be totally variant from that they had industriously propagated, and amused the public with. The uniting the civil and military offices in the same persons, too, must be conclusive to every thinking one, that there is to be but little negotiation of the civil kind." *Washington to the President of Congress*, 22 July, 1776.

for

for myself, that I would not even ask so much.— Different men will judge differently with respect to this conduct, on the part of Great Britain; I own I am bewildered and puzzled to account for it. After such an astonishing expense as they have been at, and with such fair prospects as they have before them of being soon in a capacity to prescribe their own terms, it certainly is extraordinary to find them condescending to be friends with us, on conditions as mortifying and degrading to them, as they are flattering to us. I can account for it but in one way; I really ascribe it to their magnanimity. It must be an unpleasing contest to the nation: I say the nation; for, however expedient it may be for us to have it called a ministerial war, no man who knows anything of the English government, can imagine, that the ministry could have moved a step in it, if it had not been the sense of the nation. It must, too, be a most fruitless, and unprofitable war; since every advantage they can gain, must in fact be a loss, as being gained over themselves. No wonder, therefore, they have been slow and backward to enter into it; no wonder they would be glad to be well rid of it, on almost any terms. I have ever been of this opinion, and it was this persuasion alone that reconciled me to the measure of taking up arms. I see, however, the world around me viewing it in a different light: every concession that is made

made to us, they attribute to timidity only, and despondency. I own appearances make for this conjecture; and, no doubt, Congress will give it its sanction.

I have not adopted this opinion, that we might have peace with Great Britain on terms which would, once, have been thought most honourable, on slight grounds. Yesterday, a letter was brought to me, making overtures for a negotiation, from Lord Howe.*—I had expected it; and had my instructions. It was addressed as I had foreseen, to me in my private character only. On the ground of independency, if we chose to maintain it, this was not a mere matter of punctilio: it was the critical moment of trial, whether we would assert, or recede from our pretensions. Never did men sit in debate on a question of higher magnitude: and, when they had once determined to declare their country free, I see not why they might not support this their declaration, by this as well as other means. A contrary conduct would certainly have indicated some want of firmness. Yet I confess to you, I felt awkward upon the occasion. The punctilio seemed, and it could not

---

* "July 14th a flag of truce from the fleet appeared, on which Colonel Reed and myself went down to meet it. About half way between Governor's and Staten Island, Lieutenant Brown of the Eagle offered a letter from Lord Howe, directed to 'George Washington, Esq.,' which on account of its direction we refused to receive, and parted with the usual compliments." *Diary of Samuel B. Webb*, one of Washington's aids.

but

but seem, to be my own: and as such it looked, methought, as though I were proud of my titles. Put yourself in my place; and see me, longing as you know I do most earnestly for peace, yet turning my back on a gentleman, whom I had reason to consider as the harbinger of it, only because he asked for *Mr.* and not, *General Washington*. How often it is my lot to find it my indispensible duty to act a part contrary to both my own sentiments and inclination. But, if I mistake not, it is in such instances only, that, properly speaking, we manifest our fortitude and magnanimity.*

* " About three o'clock this afternoon I was informed that a flag from Lord Howe was coming up, and waited with two of our whale-boats until directions should be given. I immediately convened such of the general officers as were not upon other duty, who agreed in opinion, that I ought not to receive any letter directed to me as a private gentleman; but if otherwise, and the officer desired to come up to deliver the letter himself, as was suggested, he should come under a safe-conduct. Upon this, I directed Colonel Reed to go down and manage the affair under the above general instruction. On his return he informed me, after the common civilities, the officer acquainted him, that he had a letter from Lord Howe to Mr. Washington, which he showed under a superscription, " *To George Washington, Esq.*" Colonel Reed replied, there was no such person in the army, and that a letter intended for the General could not be received under such a direction. The officer expressed great concern, said it was a letter rather of a civil than military nature, that Lord Howe regretted he had not arrived sooner, that he (Lord Howe) had great powers. The anxiety to have the letter received was very evident, though the officer disclaimed all knowledge of its contents. However, Colonel Reed's instructions being positive, they parted. After they had got some distance, the officer with the flag again put about, and asked under what direction Mr. Washington chose to be addressed; to which Colonel Reed answered, his station was well known, and that certainly they could be at no loss how to direct to him. The officer said they knew it, and lamented it; and again repeated his wish, that the letter could be received. Colonel Reed told him a proper direction would obviate all difficulties, and that this was no new matter, the subject

I shall

I shall astonish you, when I inform you, that this first rebuff abated not the ardour of the noble commissioner. His deputy paid us a second visit, and vouchsafed to honour me with the appellation of *General.* What name will you give to this condescension? I own it hurt me; and has well nigh led me into a train of thinking very different from all my former opinions. The gentleman, who brought the message, is a Colonel Patterson, Adjutant-General, and a sensible well-informed man.* He requested to speak to me alone; and I was glad

having been fully discussed in the course of the last year, of which Lord Howe could not be ignorant; upon which they parted.

"I would not upon any occasion sacrifice essentials to punctilio; but in this instance, the opinion of others concurring with my own, I deemed it a duty to my country and my appointment, to insist upon that respect, which, in any other than a public view, I would willingly have waived. Nor do I doubt, but, from the supposed nature of the message, and the anxiety expressed, they will either repeat their flag, or fall upon some mode to communicate the import and consequence of it." *Washington to the President of Congress,* 14 July, 1776.

On considering this subject, Congress passed the following resolution:— "That General Washington, in refusing to receive a letter said to be sent from Lord Howe, and addressed to '*George Washington, Esq.,*' acted with a dignity becoming his station; and, therefore, this Congress do highly approve the same, and do direct, that no letter or message be received, on any occasion whatsoever, from the enemy, by the Commander-in-chief, or others, the commanders of the American army, but such as shall be directed to them in the characters they respectively sustain." *Journals of Congress,* 17 July, 1776.

* Here the writer's cleverness fails him. The second message from Howe was sent on the 17th of July, and it was not until the 19th that a flag of truce came asking that the British "Adjutant General might be admitted to an interview with his Excellency General Washington," and permission being granted, Colonel Patterson came on the 20th—or four days after the above letter is supposed to have been written.

he

he did.* After the first salutations, he told me the purport of the letter which had been refused; and his errand now was to ask me to point out the most eligible means of opening a negociation, for the purpose of accommodating the unhappy dispute. I replied, that I knew but one way, and that was, by application to Congress. He said, the King's Commissioners would have no objection to treating with the members who composed the Congress, provided only that that they came with legal authority from the regular legislatures of their respective countries. I answered, they, doubtless, would come with such authority; as indeed, they could come with no other. I evidently saw his drift in the exception, as he did mine: and so put a stop to all possibility of mistake; he declared it impossible for his masters ever to acknowledge the Congress, as such, a legal and constitutional body of men, and as it seemed to be rather a punctilio of pride, than of any real importance, he hoped it might be waved. I stared: How, Sir, have you not already acknowledged the powers of Congress, by acknowledging the honourable rank I hold, and which I hold from them, and them only? That said he, was the concession merely of politeness; and made for the purpose

---

*Col. Reed and several of the general officers were present during the interview, which was held at Colonel Knox's quarters, where the General attended with his suite and life guards. *Webb.*

only

only of getting access to me: and he was persuaded, I was too sensible a man to lay any stress on so mere a trifle. I thanked him for his compliment, but assured him, that I meant to lay the most serious stress on it. If he really had that opinion of my understanding which he was pleased then to express, he must have supposed, that though a trifle in itself, it ceased to be so after I had made a point of it. Words could not have told him more strongly that our resolutions were to assert and maintain our independency. And if the Commissioners of the King of Great Britain found themselves either unable or unwilling to give up this, as a preliminary article, they, and he must pardon me for saying, that I could but think them very idly employed in soliciting an interview with me. On this, he prepared to take his leave; first adding, with a degree of sharpness and animation, that I own affected me—Sir, said he, you are pleased to be cavalier with me: I consider you as a well-meaning—I wish I could say, well-informed man; yet, I am mistaken, if your head, as well as your heart, would not, at this moment, dictate a very different language. There may be heroism, for ought I know, in desperately resolving to go all lengths with the men with whom you have connected yourself; but it is madness: and you may be thankful if posterity gives no worse name to a man who has no judgment of his own.

Wrong,

Wrong, Sir, your judgment no longer. We certainly stooped as low as the proudest wrong-head among you could ask us: but, if you really think as you seem to affect to do, that we have made these overtures either from meanness, from a distrust of our cause, or our ability to make good our just claims, you are out in all your reckoning. That the mean and narrow-minded leaders of your councils may disseminate such opinions, in your unhappy country, I can easily suppose; but remember Sir, you, and your party, owe some account to the world; and when the world shall come to know your infatuated insolence in this instance before us, as know it they must, think how you will excuse yourselves? I replied with no less warmth, nor, I trust, dignity. I was, indeed, stung: for after once having owned me as a General, you must confess there was something singularly contemptuous in presuming to school me. A few personal civilities put an end to the conference.

I have transmitted a faithful account of it to Congress; but as I can hardly suppose, they will judge it expedient to make it public, I thought I owed to you, not wholly to disappoint your curiosity. You will not, however, need me to caution you to be secret, as well on this as on other things, which I write to you.*

---

*Congress did print the report of the conversation, which was transmitted by Washington in his letter of the 22nd, and it was not until the

One

One thing more I must not omit to mention to you. In my conference with Colonel Patterson, I thought I could discover that it was intended I should be impressed with a persuasion that the

27th that it was made public. That the version in the spurious letter may be compared with that which received Washington's official endorsement, I print the latter in full.

PHILADELPHIA, July 27, 1776.

The following is an exact state of what passed at the interview between his Excellency General Washington and Colonel Patterson, Adjutant General of the army under General Howe, July 20, 1776.

After usual compliments, in which, as well as through the whole conversation, Colonel Patterson addressed General Washington by the title of Excellency, Col. Patterson entered upon the business by saying that General Howe much regretted the difficulties which had arisen respecting the address of the letters to General Washington; that it was deemed consistent with propriety, and founded upon precedents of the like nature by Ambassadors and Plenipotentiaries where disputes or difficulties of rank had arisen; that General Washington might recollect he had, last summer, addressed a letter to General Howe, To the Hon. William Howe, Esq.; that Lord Howe and General Howe did not mean to derogate from the respective rank of General Washington; that they held his person and character in the highest esteem ; that the direction, with the addition of &c. &c. &c. implied everything that ought to follow. He then produced a letter which he did not directly offer to General Washington, but observed that it was the same letter which had been sent, and laid it on the table, with a superscription to George Washington, &c. &c. &c. The General declined the letter, and said, that a letter directed to a person in a public character, should have some description or indication of it, otherwise it would appear a mere private letter; that it was true the &c. &c. &c. implied everything, and they also implied anything; that the letter to General Howe alluded to, was an answer to one received under a like address from him, which the officer on duty having taken, he did not think proper to return, but answered in the same mode of address; that he should absolutely decline any letter directed to him as a private person, when it related to his public station. Colonel Patterson then said, that General Howe would not urge his delicacy further, and repeated his assertions, that no failure of respect was intended. He then said he would endeavor, as well as he could, to recollect General Howe's sentiments on the letter and resolves of Congress, sent him a few days before, respecting the treatment of our prisoners in Canada. "That the affairs of Canada were in another department, not subject to the control of General Howe, but that he and Lord Howe utterly

Commissioners

Commissioners thought not unfavourably of our pretensions, as urged in the beginning of the dispute. This is to be accounted for. They are Whigs; and, if I am rightly informed, the General

disapproved of every infringement of the rights of humanity." Colonel Patterson then took a paper out of his pocket; and, after looking it over, said he had expressed nearly the words. General Washington then said that he had also forwarded a copy of the resolves to General Burgoyne. To which Colonel Patterson replied he did not doubt a proper attention would be paid to them, and that he (General Washington) was sensible that cruelty was not the characteristic of the British nation. Colonel Patterson then proceeded to say that he had it in charge to mention the case of General Prescott, who, they were informed, was treated with such rigor, that, under his age and infirmities, fatal consequences might be apprehended.

General Washington replied that General Prescott's treatment had not fallen under his notice; that all persons under his particular directions, he had treated with kindness, and made their situation as easy and comfortable as possible; that he did not know where General Prescott was, but believed his treatment very different from their information. General Washington then mentioned the case of Colonel Allen, and the officers who had been confined in Boston gaol. As to the first, Colonel Patterson answered that General Howe had no knowledge of it but by information from General Washington, and that the Canada department was not under his direction or control; that as to the other prisoners at Boston, whenever the state of the army at Boston admitted it, they were treated with humanity and even indulgence; that he asserted this upon his honor, and should be happy in an opportunity to prove it.

General Washington then observed, that the conduct of several of the officers would well have warranted a different treatment from what they had received; some having refused to give any parole, and others having broke it when given, by escaping or endeavoring so to do. Colonel Patterson answered, that as to the first, they misunderstood the matter very much, and seemed to have mistook the line of propriety exceedingly; and as to the latter, General Howe utterly disapproved and condemned their conduct.

That if a remonstrance was made, such violations of good faith would be severely punished; but that he hoped General Washington was too just to draw public inferences from the misbehaviour of some private individuals; that bad men were to be found in every class and society; and that such behavior was considered as a dishonor to the British army. Col. Patterson then proceeded to say, that the goodness and benevolence of the King had

owes

owes his seat in Parliament to the interest of the Dissenters.* But why approve of our first pretensions only? Surely if we were then right, we are not now wrong: I mean as to what we have a right to, by the principles of the constitution; the expediency of our measures is now out of question. I cannot dissociate the idea between our having a right of resistance in the case of taxation, and the

---

induced him to appoint Lord Howe and General Howe his commissioners, to accommodate this unhappy dispute, that they had great powers, and would derive the greatest pleasure from effecting an accommodation; and that he (Colonel Patterson) wished to have this visit considered as making the first advances to this desirable object. General Washington replied, he was not vested with any powers on this subject by those from whom he derived his authority and power. But from what had appeared or transpired on this head, Lord Howe and General Howe were only to grant pardons; that those who had committed no fault wanted no pardon, that we were only defending what we deemed our indisputable right Colonel Patterson said that would open a very wide field for argument. He then expressed his apprehensions that an adherence to forms was likely to obstruct business of the greatest moment and concern.

He then observed that a proposal had been formerly made of exchanging Governor Skene for Mr. Lovell; that he now had authority to accede to to that proposal. General Washington replied, that the proposition had been made by the direction of Congress, and having been then rejected, he could not now renew the business, or give any answer, till he had previously communicated it to them.

Colonel Patterson behaved with the greatest attention and politeness during the whole business, expressed strong acknowledgements that the usual ceremony of blinding his eyes had been dispensed with. At the breaking up of the conference, General Washington strongly invited him to partake of a small collation provided for him, which he politely declined, alledging his late breakfast, and an impatience to return to General Howe, though he had not executed his commission so amply as he wished. Finding he did not propose staying, he was introduced to the general officers, after which he took his leave, and was safely conducted to his own boat, which waited for him about four miles distant from the city. Made public by order of Congress.

* Howe was a member of the opposition.

same

same right in the case of legislating for us. You know I am no deep casuist in political speculations, but having happily been brought up in revolution principles, I thought I trod surely when I traced the footsteps of those venerable men. Wonderful! These too are the principles of our opponents; so that all our misfortune and fault is the having put in practice the very tenets which they profess to embrace.

But, I shall exhaust your patience; which I should not do, foreseeing as I do, that I shall, hereafter, have occasion to put it to the trial.

I am, with the truest regard,
    Dear Lund, Yours, &c,
        G. W.

TO LUND WASHINGTON.

NEW YORK, July 22, 1776.

I wish I could say I thoroughly approved of all the new regulations in the new institution of government in my native state. It could, however, hardly have been expected that a reformation so capital and comprehensive should be perfect at first; the wonder is, it is not still more exceptionable. My heart glows with unusual warmth when I advert, as I often do, to that pure and disinterested ardor which must have animated the bulk of my countrymen throughout the whole of this controversy. There may be exceptions amongst us, and no doubt, there are; but it is not fair to infer this from our uncommon impetuosity and violence. This one would wish restrained, but, by no means extirpated; for is it not the effect of a highly agitated spirit: the mere effervescence of good principles thrown into a state of strong fermentation? And surely, even precipitancy is preferable to the spirit-breaking cautions of chill despondency. Yet I am no advocate, in general, either for rash measures, or rash men; but at such a conjuncture as this, men had need to be stimulated by some more active

active principle than cool and sober reason. They must be enthusiasts, or they will continue to be slaves.*

I give this in answer to my friend Mr. Carter's† objections to the first procedures of the new government. No doubt, Henry is, in many respects, the unfittest man in the State for Governor of Virginia.‡ He has no property, no learning, but little good sense, and still less virtue or public spirit; but he is the idol of the people; and as it is by their means only that you can hope to effect the grand schemes which you have meditated,

---

*The Virginia Convention met at Williamsburg, May 6th, and remained in session until July 5th. Of what was done, Edmund Randolph, a member, wrote: "Everything which had been done in the Convention of May was hailed as masterpieces of political wisdom, and acted upon with a cheerfulness and submission which naturally resulted from the first demonstration of popular self-government. The young boasted that they were treading upon the republican ground of Greece and Rome, and contracted a sovereign contempt for British institutions. With them to recede from those institutions with abomination was the perfection of political philosophy. Not a murmur was heard against the competency of the Convention to frame the constitution according to its full extent. Nay, so captivating were its charms, that it was many years before some of its defects, even upon the theory of democracy itself, were allowed or detected." Quoted in Conway, *Edmund Randolph*, 32.

† Landon Carter.

‡ Henry was chosen governor by 60 votes; 45 were cast for Nelson, and 1 for Page. Henry had incurred the enmity of the "aristocratic" element in Virginia, men of wealth and landed estates, who controlled the leading offices in the State during colonial rule. "I think my countrymen made a capital mistake when they took Henry out of the Senate to place him in the field; and pity it is, that he does not see this and remove every difficulty by a voluntary resignation." *Washington to Joseph Reed*, 7 March, 1776.

"I congratulate you, Sir, most cordially, upon your appointment to the government. . . . Your correspondence will confer honor and satisfaction." *Washington to Governor Henry*, 5 October, 1776.

you

you must honor them, and indulge them with their rattle. They will soon tire of him; and the opportunity must then be watched gently to lead them to a better choice; for they may be led, though they cannot be driven. And though it be alas! but too true, that they often mistake their real interests; I am of opinion they never mistake them long. Sooner or later, they will judge and act from their settled feelings, and these I take it are generally founded in their settled interests. When great enterprises are to be performed, we may well dispense with some errors in judgment; when without that, we have, in its stead, that which perhaps we could not have with it; I mean, that undisciplined ardor which is infinitely better adapted to our purposes.

There cannot be a more striking instance that the judgment of the people may, in general, be safely trusted, in the long run, than is to be met with in Virginia. Very few countries have to boast of more men of respectable understandings; I know of none that can produce a family, all of them distinguished as clever men, like our Lees.* They are all of them the very men one would wish

---

* At this time two of the family—Richard Henry, and Francis Lightfoot—were members of the Continental Congress; Arthur and William were in Europe, soon to take a prominent part in diplomatic relations between the United States and France; and Thomas Ludwell was a member of the Virginia Convention from Stafford. In the list of members occur, also, the names Henry Lee (of Prince William) and Richard Lee (of Westmoreland).

for

for to take the lead of a willing multitude; for they are certainly men of shining talents, and their talents are of that particular kind which usually render men popular. No men are more so, than the men in question once were. It is obvious, this is no longer the case; and the reason must be that they are no longer worthy of it. With all their cleverness they are selfish in the extreme. The people, at length, found this out; or, no doubt, R. H. Lee would have now been governor, the grand object of all his aims.*

You would be mortified to hear the criticisms which are common here on Henry's inauguration speech.† It is, indeed, a poor and pitiful performance; and yet I can believe that set off by his smooth and oily delivery, it would appear clever when he spoke it. Why did he not ask Mr. Page to prepare it for him? There is not a man in America more capable,‡ The Counsellors of State are certainly irreproachable, and will do honor to those who appointed them.§ I am particularly pleased with the success of my honest brother-in-

---

* The more probable cause of Lee's not being better recognized is given by John Adams, *Works*, III, 31.

† Printed in Force, *American Archives, Fourth Series*, VI, 1602.

‡ Probably John Page, or his half brother, Mann Page.

§ The Privy Council was to be composed of John Page, Dudley Digges, John Tayloe, John Blair, Benjamin Harrison of Berkeley, Bartholomew Dandridge, Thomas Nelson, and Charles Carter of Shirley. As Nelson could not serve, Benjamin Harrison of Brandon was chosen in his place.

law

law Bat Dandridge:* and the pleasure is not lessened, by the assurance he makes me, that my letters were serviceable to him, there being but few men whom I love more than I do him. As you are soon to go down the country, you will see him; and therefore spare me the trouble of writing particularly to him. My friends must now be so indulgent to me, as to wave the matter of compliment: I think myself happy, whenever I can write, as I should on urgent business. You know how ticklish my situation is: little as one would think there is to be envied in it, I yet am envied. And though, in all good reason, their fears should take a direct contrary course, there are who are for ever suggesting suspicions and jealousies of the army and its commander. My own heart assures me I mean them no ill: however if I really have the influence and ascendency which they suppose, I will for their sakes as well as my own, hereafter maintain it at some little cost. A thousand considerations determine me to strain every nerve to prevent the army's being under any other control whilst I live. Let a persuasion of the necessity of this, if occasion should arise, be seasonably urged in my native state; and in the mean while, let some more than ordinary pains be taken to make me popular. Their own honor and interest are both concerned in my being

---

* Bartholomew Dandridge was brother of Mrs. Washington.

SO.

so. Shew this to Mr. Dandridge; and as you both can enter into my meaning, even from the most distant hints, I can rest satisfied that you will do everything I wish you.

We have lately had a general review; and I have much pleasure in informing you, that we made a better appearance, and went thorough our exercises more like soldiers than I had expected. The Southern states are rash and blamable in the judgment they generally form of their brethren of the four New England states; I do assure you, with all my partiality for my own countrymen, and prejudices against them, I cannot but consider them as the flower of the American Army. They are a strong, vigorous, and hardy people, inured to labor and toil; which our people seldom are. And though our hot and eager spirits may, perhaps, suit better in a sudden and desperate enterprise; yet in the way in which wars are now carried on, you must look for permanent advantages only from that patient and persevering temper, which is the result of a life of labor. The New Englanders are cool, considerate, and sensible; whilst we are all fire and fury: like their climate, they maintain an equal temperature, whereas we cannot shine, but we burn. They have a uniformity and stability of character, to which the people of no other states have any pretension; hence they must and will always preserve their influence in this great Empire.

Empire.* Were it not for the drawbacks and the disadvantages, which the influence of their popular opinions, on the subject of government, have over their army, they soon might, and probably would, give law to it. If General Putnam had the talents of Mr. S. Adams, or Mr. Adams had his, perhaps, even at this moment, this had not been matter of conjecture. But Putnam is a plain, blunt, undesigning old fellow, whose views reach no further than the duties of his profession; he is, indeed, very ignorant,† yet I find him a useful officer; and chiefly because he neither plagues me nor

---

* From the first there was this jealousy between the New England troops and those of the other colonies. The truth seems to have been that the ideas of equality that were prevalent among the former found little sympathy among the latter. Numerous quotations could be made to prove this; but one is given, from a letter of Washington to Patrick Henry, 5 October, 1776: "One circumstance, in this important business, ought to be cautiously guarded against, and that is, the soldiers and officers being too nearly on a level. Discipline and subordination add life and vigor to military movements. The person commanded yields but a reluctant obedience to those, who he conceives are undeservedly made his superiors, The degrees of rank are frequently transferred from civil life into the departments of the army. The true criterion to judge by, when past services do not enter into the competition, is, to consider whether the candidate for office has just pretension to the character of a gentleman, a proper sense of honor, and some reputation to lose.

"Perhaps, Sir, you may be surprised at my pressing this advice so strongly as I have done in this letter; but I have felt the inconveniences resulting from a contrary principle in so sensible a manner, and this army has been so greatly enfeebled by a different line of conduct, that I hope you will readily excuse me."

† That Putnam was a "very ignorant" man may be seen by an order issued by him when in command at Philadelphia in December 1776: "All ofisors and solders boath Thoas that are Newly inlisted into the contenentol sarwis. Thos of the flieing camp the melishey and all the Inhabitence of this City are requested to parad to-morrow moruing at 9 o'clock at the

others.

others, with wrangling claims of privileges. I owe him too, no small acknowledgments, for the fairness of his accounts. I could open to you some strange scenes in this way. Some people seem to have gotten such a habit of cheating government, that, though sufficiently conscientious in other respects, they really are far less scrupulous in their manner of charging than, I think, becomes them. —But as I have often told you, General Mercer is the man, on whom these states must rest their hopes. The character that one of his countrymen gave to the Pretender, fits him exactly: "He is the most cautious man I ever saw, not to be a coward; and the bravest, not to be rash." In my judgment, he is not inferior to General Lee, in military knowledge; and in almost everything else, he is, infinitely, his superior. Yet the overbearing virtues of this last named gentleman are useful to us, especially at our setting out: we wanted not the sober and slow deductions of argument and reason; and Lee, like the author of Common Sense, has talents perfectly formed to dazzle and confound.*

Markit to go on fitig to fortify this city and so on Every morning til farther orders.

ISRAEL PUTNAM."

This order, quoted by Dawson, as written by Putnam, may, however, have been written by some adjutant whose spelling was somewhat eccentric. Washington did not hold Putnam's military merits in any high esteem.

* General Lee "is the first officer, in military knowledge and experience, I thank

I thank you for your care in making the remittances you mention to Messrs. Carey & Co.* I sincerely wish they may arrive safe; as I certainly owe it to them to take every step in my power to make them easy. There is a pleasure in doing as one ought, in little as well as great affairs; but, in my present circumstances, I should often want this pleasure, were it not for your affectionate assiduity, and truly friendly attention. God bless you, my dear friend, for every instance of your care and concern for me.

I am, &c—
G. W.

---

we have in the whole army. He is zealously attached to the cause, honest and well meaning, but rather fickle and violent, I fear, in his temper." *Washington to his brother*, 31 March, 1776.

*Robert Cary and Company were Washington's factors in London. To them he sent the bulk of his tobacco shipments, and through them he obtained all the supplies that the plantation needed and which could not be made or purchased in America.

APPENDIX.

THE CAREY COLLECTION OF THE "OFFICIAL LETTERS."

JOHN CAREY, LL. D.*

"Classical scholar, brother of Mathew Carey, author of the 'Vindiciæ Hibernicæ,' and of William Paulet Carey, was born in Ireland in 1756. At the age of twelve he was sent to finish his education in a French university. He spent some time in the United States about 1789, and afterwards passed many years in London as a teacher of the classics, French, and shorthand. He died at Prospect Place, Lambeth, 8 Dec., 1826, from calculus, the last years of his life having been embittered by distressing complaints.

"Carey was editor of the early numbers of the 'School Magazine,' published by Phillips, and a frequent contributor to the 'Monthly' and 'Gentleman's' Magazines. In the former journal in 1803 he made a suggestion for enabling persons on shore to give assistance to distressed vessels by means of shooting a wooden ball from a mortar, an idea subsequently conceived and carried out independently by Captain G. M. Manby, for which invention Manby was rewarded by government.

---

*From Leslie Stephen's *Dictionary of National Biography*.

government. Carey brought out a new edition of Dryden's 'Virgil,' 1803, 3 vols., 8vo, and again in 1819, two editions of Ainsworth's 'Latin Dictionary' in 4to, and five of the abridgment of the same; the 'Gradus ad Parnassum' in 1824; the Latin 'Common Prayer' in Bagster's polyglot edition; 'Ruperti commentarius in Livium,' and a revision of Schleusner's 'New Testament Lexicon' (1826). He likewise edited more than fifty volumes of the 'Regent Latin Classics' published by Baldwin. He was the compiler of the valuable 'General Index to the Monthly Review from 1790 to 1816' (2 vols., 1818), and translated Bitaubé's 'Batavians,' Madame de Staël's 'Young Emigrants,' Lehmen's 'Letters on Switzerland,' and others, In 1810 he published a story for children called 'Learning better than House and Land,' which went through several editions. His school-books were popular in their day and generally praised for accuracy and scholarly qualities. Among them are: 1. Latin Prosody made easy,' 1800; new edition 1812. 2. 'Practical English Prosody and Versification,' 1809. 3. 'Alphabetic Key to the Propria quæ maribus,' 1812. 4. 'Introduction to English Composition and Elocution,' 1817. 5. 'Clavis Metrico Virgiliana,' 1818. 6. 'Eton Latin Prosody illustrated,' 1818. 7. 'Greek Terminations,' 1821. 8. 'Latin Terminations,' 1821. He published also a small volume of poems, with a portrait prefixed."—*C. W. Sutton.*

JEFFERSON TO CAREY.

Th : Jefferson presents his compliments to Mr. Carey and will with pleasure give him access to any papers of his office which no longer require secrecy. The difficulty will be how to separate these from those still requiring secrecy without giving Mr. Carey access to the whole, which Th : J. would not think himself free to do. Perhaps Mr. Carey can from the Journals of Congress, or other sources, designate the particular papers he would wish to publish. He shall be ready to confer with Mr. Carey on this subject when he pleases.

July 3, 1792.

CAREY TO JEFFERSON.

Sir : I have the honor of presenting for your inspection the remainder of what I have been able to copy of General Washington's correspondence. The whole of those 808 pages, and the best part of what has been copied by two of the gentlemen in your office, has been carefully compared with the original. One of the original letters, of a particular nature, I take the liberty of enclosing. The index, that accompanies the papers, will shew where to find my copy, if you wish to cut it out : and if this be the case, I presume I will not do amiss in striking out every passage (for several occur in other letters) pointing out even the existence of such pieces.

I

I am extremely sorry, that it is not in my power to complete the correspondence of the commander in chief, as I expect to embark on Sunday next. However, if I might, without impropriety, request your interference, I am confident that a single word from you would considerably expedite the business, and induce the two gentlemen in your office to hasten the part they have in hands—which was undertaken on a presumption that I was to sail by the first of April,—is already paid for in advance—and not yet finished. Indeed the difficulties and delays that have been unnecessarily thrown in my way, since I first employed an *extern* to assist me, and dropped hints that I might probably complete the work,—would render it necessary for me to request your interference in another manner, if I were to stay and continue it. But this being wholly out of my power, I think it needless to particularize them.

Before I conclude, sir, I would beg leave to remind you of the utility of a certificate, under the seal of your office, purporting in general terms that I have, under the proper authority, had access to the original papers, have made oath (which I am ready to do) that I have diligently and carefully copied, have not willingly perverted the text in any instance—and that my copies have been compared with and corrected by the originals.

As to sealing up my papers, and directing them in the manner I had the honor of mentioning to you some time ago, you alone, sir, are a competent judge of the propriety of the measure. I shall therefore duly observe (as perhaps this circumstance may make some difference)

difference) that the vessel, in which I sail, is to touch first at Lisbon, and thence, in 4 or 5 days, proceed to Dublin. With sentiments &c.
JOHN CAREY.
Tuesday, April 23, 1793.

CAREY TO WASHINGTON.

Sir: By the Ship Factor, Captain Bowen, I have the honor of transmitting to Your Excellency two copies of your letters to Congress, written during the first four years of that memorable contest, which, under your auspices, so happily terminated in the establishment of American Independence.

If, in any passage, I have mistaken your sense,—if, by any errors of the press, it is obscured,—permit me, sir, to hope that such mistakes will be excused, when with great truth I declare, that I have used my best endeavors to guard against them, and intend to rectify in a second edition whatever I can discover to be wrong in the first.

Respecting the plan of publication that I have adopted, which I fear Your Excellency will at first sight disapprove, and which is far from being satisfactory to myself,—I would beg leave to refer to one of the copies above mentioned,—the one in boards,—containing some manuscript remarks expressive of the motives that influenced me on the occasion.*

---

* I was in hopes that this copy might be among the Washington books in the Boston Athenæum; but an inquiry addressed to Mr. Cutter, the courteous librarian, brought out the fact that it was not in that collection.

With sincere and ardent wishes for Your Excellency's health, and that the indulgence of heaven may long preserve you a blessing to that happy Country which is so much indebted to you for the happiness it enjoys,—I have the honor to be
Your Excellency's most obedient humble servant,
JOHN CAREY.
London, March 31, 1795.

CAREY TO JEFFERSON.

Sir : I do myself the honor of transmitting you two volumes of those official documents, which, through your favor and indulgence, I was enabled to transcribe. I would have published two or three volumes more, had not a chasm in the General's correspondence, and the want of many of the enclosures, stopped my progress. On this subject I take the liberty of writing to Mr. Madison, Mr. Page, and Mr. Beckley, hoping, by their interposition on the spot, to have the deficiencies supplied. If successful, I shall immediately proceed, and complete the work as soon as possible.

Here I beg leave to observe, that, recollecting your caution respecting the premature publication of certain passages, I have endeavored to pursue the path you had marked out, and to keep clear of everything which might, at the present day, have an unpleasing tendency. Had I printed in Philadelphia, I should have been less scrupulous: there, any unlucky slips could have been attributed only to inadvertence: whereas, now

now that I live under a government radically hostile to the Union, they might, by the American reader, be imputed to sinister motives on my part,—and possibly give rise to some invective against even you, sir, for having, though with the most laudable intentions, countenanced the publication. And, though perfectly convinced that such obloquy were incapable of disturbing a mind like yours, I was nevertheless unwilling that my conduct should furnish the theme; and preferred injuring the sale of the book by the omission ot many passages which would have been read with avidity on this side the Atlantic.

JOHN CAREY.

London, April 7, 1795.

CAREY TO WASHINGTON.

LONDON, 8 SEPTEMBER, 1796.

Sir: When you consider the serious nature of the business on which I have the honor to address you, I trust your good sense will induce you to overlook and excuse any impropriety or indelicacy which there may be in my writing to you on the subject. A few days since I, for the first time, saw a book entitled "Epistles Domestic &c. from General Washington." As you also have probably seen it, I need not describe its contents. On reading it, I felt what every honest man must feel, indignation and contempt for the anonymous editor.

Happening luckily to be acquainted with some of the gentlemen who write for the critical Review, I requested

quested an indulgence which I scorned to ask last year when my own interests were concerned (*i. e.* on the publication of the two volumes of your official Letters)—I requested and obtained permission to write a critique of the volume in question. I have the honor of inclosing it, for your *own private inspection* only, until it appears in print—which will be on the first of October, with perhaps some alterations or amendments, if any occur in the interim between this first hasty expression of my thoughts, and my seeing the proof sheets. As soon as published I shall do myself the honor of transmitting a printed copy of the Review that contains it.

I regret extremely that I cannot (without openly avowing myself the author), point out to the public the prodigious incorrectness of Mr. Duche's letter. Having compared it with a correct copy which I have taken from the files, I find no less than *one hundred and forty* deviations from the genuine text:—in which number I do not count orthography and punctuation.

Permit me, Sir, to add that I am much at a loss to know whether I ought openly to take any notice of this affair in case I should publish a continuation of your "Official Letters;" which I wish to do as soon as I can make it convenient. Perhaps some means may be found to guide my feeble and fallible judgment. I wish to act for the best; and if, Sir, the uprightness of my intention will, I trust, excuse me. I take it for granted that Mr. Randolph has informed your Excellency of my intention respecting the whole letters and passages of letters which I have omitted in my former publication—which is (as I informed him in two letters
written

written in November last) not to publish them during your Excellency's lifetime—nor even afterwards, if deemed unadvisable by persons on whose judgment and integrity I can rely.

I shall shortly take the liberty of waiting on Mr. King, who may perhaps be able to furnish me with some useful advice—though I do not mean to inform him of my being the writer of the critique. * * *

JOHN CAREY.

On the wrapper is written in Carey's *MS*:

"This letter not having any relation to public affairs, and not being written to the President *as* President of the U. S., but intended for General Washington in his private capacity—is not to be opened by his secretary, or by any other person than himself."

[ENCLOSURE.]

When this volume before us first came to our hands, we took it up with avidity, expecting that it no doubt contained the promised continuation of, or the appendix to, the two interesting volumes of General Washington's genuine and authentic letters, of which we gave our readers an account last year. But we were soon undeceived by the following anonymous account of the manner in which these papers are said to have been obtained—

[Here is inserted the preface to the spurious letters.]

The recollection of the Shakesperian trunk being yet recent in our mind, we smiled at the idea of the Mulatto's budget; and not immediately adverting to the tendency of the concluding words of the above extract, we expected nothing worse than that the contents of Billy's portmanteau were merely the production of some sportive genius who chose to indulge his fancy in embellishing facts with the charms of characteristic and probable fiction, for the purpose of amusing his readers and benefitting himself, without injury to his neighbor. Under this idea we proceeded to the perusal of the volume with a resolution of deriving from it as much pleasure and entertainment as it is capable of affording. But we had not read many pages ere we found reasons to alter our opinions, and to suspect that the design of the anonymous fabricator was no very laudable one:—a
suspicion

suspicion which was fully confirmed before we reached the end of the book, and in which we believe the majority of our readers will concur, when they have accompanied us in our examination of its contents.

The volume consists of two parts—the letters said to have been found in the mulatto fellow's possession, and an appendix. The former fill sixty-two pages, and are seven in number, viz: one to Mrs. Washington, one to Mr. Custis, and five to Mr. Lund Washington—containing no details of the war, no development of the secret causes of events—but chiefly filled up with the doubts, anxieties, and vague apprehensions of the supposed writer, intermingled with some private matter of an uninteresting nature, but all together serving as a convenient vehicle for a few remarkable passages which we shall presently lay before our readers, as they are the marrow and quintessence of the whole—the rest being in fact "naught but leather and penuells." But it is necessary that we first take some notice of the appendix, as it is there we can more certainly find a clue to unravel the anonymous editor's design.

From page 100 to 227, we are presented with various pieces respecting the treatment of the American prisoners—proposals for an exchange, letters from the British commanders urging General Washington to accede to the measure, proceedings of the commissioners met for that purpose, refusal of the British commissioner to consent to a partial exchange, viz: that of officers only, with various other papers all tending to the same end, which is, to show that the Americans avoided an exchange, from motives of "cruel and unjustifiable policy;" and these are sufficiently explained by a short hint (page 150) at the different value of the British troops who were enlisted for life, and the American soldiers whose time of service was expired or expiring, and who would immediately on their release return to their firesides, instead of swelling the continental army, to oppose the accession of strength which their enemies had acquired by the exchange; that the Congress was influenced by such considerations, is pretty certain; and the consequences were grievously complained of at the time by the unfortunate sufferers and their friends, and are to this day remembered with indignation. But General Washington ever reprobated such policy; and accordingly we find him (in his Official Letters, vol ii, pp. 235 et seq.) combating it with all the glow of language and energy of argument which the honest indignation of a generous heart and tender sympathy for the sufferings of his gallant compatriots, could inspire. In the publication before us, however, the unwary reader is taught to impute the whole blame to him alone, since a resolution of Congress is produced (p, 104) *seemingly* giving him full power to treat for a general exchange. But in comparing the resolution with the printed Journals of Congress, we find that the anonymous editor has falsified it, to answer his own purposes. And, lest we should attribute his faux-pas in this instance to a casual error of the press, the same falsification is again repeated in two other places (pp. 110 and 115), where that part of the resolution is quoted. According to him, Congress

gress are made to say, that "if . . . all the officers of the enemy shall be exchanged, and a balance of *prisoners* remain in their hands, then an equivalent *of privates* shall be settled;" whereas Congress themselves say (Journals, Vol. iv, p. 666) "a balance of *officers*" and an equivalent of *privates, to be given in exchange for such officers*—it being in fact their wish to redeem their officers only and to release as few privates of the British troops as possible: with which view, they effectually tied up their general's hands by the resolution in question, and put it out of his power to treat for a general exchange.

From page 227 to 254, we have the proceedings of the American army in 1783 to obtain a redress of grievances;—viz, anonymous summons for a meeting of officers, address exciting the troops to revolt, general orders on the occasion, for convening a meeting of officers "to hear the report of the committee from the army to Congress; second anonymous address, proceedings of the regular authorized meeting, with General Washington's address to them. These pieces are copied from the printed Journals of Congress, (for it is to be observed that the General gave that body early information of the whole business), and appear to have been solely introduced for the sake of the following passage in the second anonymous address, which seems to point him out as a favorer, at least, if not the prime instigator, of the mutiny, for purposes which must be obvious to every reader. The words within crotchets, in this and the following extracts, are the true readings, which we have copied from the Journals (Vol. viii, pp. 233 et seq.), though some of the deviations from the text are of little moment, except so far as they may enable us to form an opinion of the editor's fidelity in other instances where we have not an opportunity of detecting him.

"The general order of yesterday, which the weak may mistake for disapprobation, and the designing dare to represent as such, wears, in my opinion, a very different complexion, and *carries with it a very dangerous tendency* [*carries with it a very opposite tendency*]. Till now, the commander in chief has regarded the steps you have taken for redress, with good wishes alone. This *official* [ostensible] silence has authorized your meetings, and his private *opinions* [*opinion has*] sanctified your claim. Had he disliked the object in view, would not the same sense of duty which forbade you from meeting *on the third and sevenths?* [*on the third day of the week, have forbidden you from meeting on the seventh ?*] Is not the same object held up for your discussion? And has it not passed the seal of office, and taken the solemnity of an order? This will give system to your proceedings, and stability to your resolves. It will ripen speculation into fact; and while it adds to the unanimity, it *cannot lessen* [*cannot possibly lessen*] the independence of your sentiments." p. 239.

In comparing the General's address to the assembled officers (p. 241) with the authentic copy in the Journals (Vol. viii, p. 244), we noticed *thirty-four* deviations from the genuine text; among which are the following: "As men

men see through difficulties [different optics] and are induced by the reflecting faculties of the mind to use different means to obtain the same end" —" If men are to be precluded from offering their sentiments on a matter which may *involve the consideration of mankind* [*involve the most serious and alarming consequences that can invite the consideration of mankind*], reason is of no use to us." The address . . . "is intended [calculated] to impress the mind with an idea of premeditated injustice *TO the sovereign power of the United States* [*IN the sovereign power of the U. S.*]"—The endeavors of Congress "to discover and establish *funds* have been unwearied" [*"funds for this purpose*," i. e. that of paying and remunerating the troops.] "So far as may be done consistently with the great duty I owe my country, and those powers *I AM bound to respect* [*WE ARE bound to respect*], you may command my services to the *utmost of* [*utmost extent*] *of* my abilities."

After these specimens of the editor's *accuracy* and of his *good will* to the illustrious character whose letters he pretends to publish, let me now return to the letters themselves, and lay before our readers the passages above alluded to,—recollecting, meanwhile, the extreme caution of the supposed writer in packing up and securing his papers previous to the evacuation of N. York (as mentioned in his Official Letters, vol. i, p. 227), and the consequent improbability that *such* a man would leave behind him, in the possession of a sick mulatto slave, *such* letters as are here ascribed to him.

[Here follow some extracts from the spurious letters.]

We have here sufficient to render any yet surviving members of the first Congress, of those who voted the declaration of independence, and all the warm abettors of this measure, hostile to the supposed writer, and to excite a thousand injurious surmises in the bosoms of those who are dissatisfied with the late commercial treaty, and who accuse the President of having sacrificed the interests of the United States to those of G. Britain. The motive attributed to him for taking the command of the army is well calculated to render the whole N. England States jealous of him, and inimical to his cause. The more effectually, however, to accomplish this latter object, we find him (p. 9) wishing to set fire to Boston, &c.—" Not without the loss of many men and much property," to cut off the British garrison— and only prevented by the selfish and interested considerations of the Massachusetts Assembly, whom he is made to represent, a little further on, as disposed cheerfully to acquiesce in the burning of N. York, and the sacrifice of the Southern regiments, without a dissentient voice. The following character which the General is made to draw of the influential family of the Lees—that of Mr. Henry, who was in fact, as here represented, the idol of Virginia—together with the remarks on the Virginia officers, are calculated to render the supposed writer unpopular even in his own state, and by natural sequence, in all the Southern States; Virginia having so decided a preponderance preponderence in that quarter, that she may very justly be termed the arbitress of the South.

We shall close our extracts with the following, which is the master stroke of the whole performance, and well adapted to excite in the reader's mind the idea of a Pisistratus, a Cæsar, or a Cromwell, especially when he compares this with the extract already given from the anonymous address to the army, and with a passage in page 60, where the General is made to treat very lightly, and even to doubt the existence of a conspiracy against him, which, however, he represented to Congress at the time as very real and serious, and which appeared in the same light to a council of general officers, who, on a full investigation of the matter, condemned one of the conspirators to death, as we learn from his Official Letters, vol. i, p. 174. "There are men who are forever suggesting . . . . everything I wish you." p. 51.

We now take our leave of the volume, with the observation (which has, no doubt, been anticipated by our readers), that, as the anonymous personage to whom the world is *indebted* for these letters, have, by his false quotations from the public journals of Congress, shewn how little dependence is to be placed on him, we hold ourselves fully justified in pronouncing the contents of the mulatto's budget to be in a very high degree apocryphal—that either the letters in question were never written by Genl. Washington, or, if he did write any such, they have been garbled, interpolated and falsified by the editor, who felt himself secure from detection in this quarter; and as, in the falsification which we have proved against him, he aimed at blackmailing the character of General Washington, we may naturally conclude that the same design pervades the whole of his performance—a performance which can, to no impartial considerate man, appear in any other light than that of an arrant forgery, trumped up for the purpose of rendering the President of the U. S. unpopular, and thus, probably, either compelling him to resign his high office in disgust, or, at least, preventing his reappointment—in short, an *electioneering manœuvre* altogether.

CAREY TO WASHINGTON.

Sir: I have the honor of transmitting to your Excellency a copy of the Critical Review, containing remarks on a publication which bears your name, as mentioned in a letter of Sept. 9, which I took the liberty of addressing to Your Excellency, by the brig Diana, Potts. At the same time I beg leave to assure
Your

Your Excellency, that, had I then known from what source the letters were derived, I should not have thought it worth while to trouble Your Excellency on the subject. To the politeness of the American Minister, Mr. King, I am indebted for my knowledge of the origin of the fabrication, which of course rendered it necessary to make many alterations from the manuscript inclosed in the letter above mentioned.

I conclude, Sir, by requesting that Your Excellency will indulgently Pardon my presumption in addressing you at all on the occasion; and believe me to be &c. &c.,

London, Oct. 1, 1796.　　　　　　JOHN CAREY.

P. S. A report, circulated here, of your Excellency's *declared* intention to retire from Public life about this time, induced me to take the precaution observable in this as well as the former packet (of Sept. 9), lest a successor, or any one else, should think himself entitled to inspect the Contents, as being addressed to the "President of the United States." Another copy of Review, with a duplicate of these lines, is forwarded by the Fame, Harris, bound for New York.

JEFFERSON TO CAREY.

MONTICELLO, 10 NOVEMBER, '96.

* * * With respect to the passages omitted in the official letters, I am totally uninformed of their nature; for tho' I received from Mr. Rice the copy you were so kind as to send me, and for which I return you my thanks,

thanks, yet, having gone over his letters in their MS. state, I have not read them as published, and indeed had I read them, it is not probable my memory would have enabled me to judge of the omissions. I am therefore prepared to give but one opinion, which is that the whole of the MSS. examined and passed by myself, and the doubtful passages referred to the President and passed by him, were proper for publication. For tho' there were passages which might on publication create uneasiness in the minds of some, and were therefore referred by me to the President, yet I concurred fully in the opinion he pronounced, that as these things were true, they ought to be known. To render history what it ought to be, the whole truth should be known. I am no friend to mystery and state secrets. They serve generally only to conceal the errors and rogueries of those who govern. I sincerely wish you may be able to prosecute your plan of publishing all the official letters of our war which may contribute to its history.

TH: JEFFERSON.

HOW WASHINGTON BECAME COMMANDER-IN-CHIEF.

[*From The Nation, June 13, 1889.*]

WASHINGTON, June 1, 1889.

It is well to review occasionally our accepted historical conceptions, gauging them by newly discovered material, and, in the clearness of vision that distance of time permits, altering the perspective, or distribution of light and shade, as the confusion of controversy subsides. The recent celebration in New York proves that the popular enthusiasm for the national hero has by no means diminished, but rather increased, in the course of a century; so that it is only just and proper to recur to the past and revise, where necessary, what have wrongly become popular ideas through carelessness, ignorance, or blind adoration. It is to the last that we are most indebted for our historical fallacies.

Washington came to the Presidency the elect of the nation. The movement that led to his selection was spontaneous, unanimous, and heartfelt—such an unquestioned tribute as has rarely been paid to any man. Without him the Constitution would not have been accepted by the States, and it was with him in their thoughts

thoughts that the Convention created the office of President, and somewhat fearfully clothed it with great powers—for jealousy of power in any national or (to use the more common phrase of that day) federal body or appointment was the bugbear of those who had been most actively engaged in the contest against royal prerogative, the cruel edicts of a corrupt Parliament, and the armies and machinations of a "wicked and abandoned" ministry. The fear and jealousy that were directed against Great Britain in 1765-82, were turned against the Congress and the advocates of a continental policy in 1783-88. It was the personality of Washington that contributed largely to bear down this jealousy; and when he journeyed to New York to assume his high office, it may be truly said that throughout the land there was not heard a voice disapproving the choice.

To read the generally accepted history of the Revolution, one would suppose that it was with a like unanimity that Washington was appointed to the command of the Continental army in 1775; that he then stepped into a position to which the universal suffrage of the colonies was calling him. Nothing could be further from the truth; and to strip the incident of all the romantic features that hero-worship has thrown around it, it may be described, in the somewhat vulgar parlance of to-day, as the result of a "political deal" got up between Massachusetts and Virginia. The result justified the wisdom of the choice, and led to much self-congratulation on the remarkable sagaciousness of Congress and the really marvellous fitness of
the

the man for the place—ideas handed down to us as remarkable instances of prescience on the part of the Congress. The fact was, and we may write it in all reverence, that Washington had not known military service since 1758; that he was better remembered for his defeat and surrender at Fort Necessity, for his pertinacious and sometimes unreasonable claims for precedence in command, and his obstinate pestering of General Forbes about the proper road to Fort Duquesne, which led Forbes to really dislike him, than for his successful mission to the Ohio in 1753, and his courage and daring under Braddock. For nearly sixteen years he had been without a command, a planter of tobacco and raiser of wheat, a successful manager of a large estate, and an eager and active speculator in Western lands.

This was not the stuff of which a military hero was made, and while in 1774 the formation of so-called independent companies throughout Virginia in a measure renewed his military prestige, it was not as a soldier that he was thought of, even in his own colony. Jonathan Boucher, the Tory preacher and tutor of Jacky Custis, who knew Washington well, did not err far when he said that the "most distinguished" part of his (W's) character was that he was an "admirable farmer;" and no one was more surprised than he to see this man, who had always acquitted himself "decently, but never greatly," develop into a great leader of armies, and, later, of the people. Edmund Randolph wrote with much truth that, at the beginning of 1774, "some others were more prominent than

than Washington. It could not have been then truly foretold that the germs of solid worth which afterwards overspread our land with illustrious fruit, would elevate him very far above many of the friends of the Revolution." While constantly chosen one of the Burgesses from his county, a position that his large estates, serving as a "pocket borough," gave him, he never attained the honor and pre-eminence of being chosen to the Governor's council — a reward that marked the happy owner as a favored one and one of the "notables." He had a wide acquaintance in Maryland, Philadelphia, and New York, and his diaries show how high these acquaintances were in the social life of their respective colonies; but his cold temperament forbade many intimate friends, and it is very doubtful if he could have been described by many of his acquaintances, or could have been recognized even by name outside of these circles. Had he nominated himself and "run" for an office. his standing would have been slight outside of his own county, and none at all outside of his colony. This is sad reading to the romancer on Washington but the facts bear out this statement of the case.

The Continental Congress of 1774 was more useful in bringing together delegates from the different colonies, and allowing an interchange of views, than for its acts and paper remonstrances. The Bostonians were much pitied throughout the land as objects of ministerial cruelty, but this sympathy was rather for their present sufferings than for what were regarded as their rash and intemperate aims, interpreted then as a
desire

desire to be independent not only of Great Britain, but of the other colonies too. Martyrdom was not considered as a good ground for conferring leadership, and a little resentment was caused by the "inward vanity and self-conceit" of the Bostonians, which led them to "assume big and haughty airs," and to "affect to dictate and take the lead in Continental measures." Wait, wrote the mild General Gage to his master, and see these Bostonians pay the other colonies "the compliment of taking their advice." His words were true. In the Congress of 1775, by their explanations and personal intercourse with the other delegates, the Massachusetts men were able to remove in a measure their reputation for rashness, and came to be "universally applauded as cool and judicious."

Among the Southern members thus influenced was Washington. His letters to Bryan Fairfax prove that he heartily sympathized with the general cause of the colonies before he attended the Congress at Philadelphia. While it was sitting, he saw somewhat of the Massachusetts delegates. On September 28 he records in his diary having dined at Edward Shippen's, and spent the afternoon with the Boston gentlemen, and Adams notes that he spent that evening at home with Colonel Lee and Colonel Washington, "who came in to consult us." On October 7, the two sets of delegates again met at Thomas Smith's. The result of these meetings is reflected in a letter Washington wrote to one of his old military companions, then in Gage's army at Boston. Though you are led to believe, he wrote in effect, that the Bostonians are rebellious

lious, setting up for independence, and what not, I know from their leaders that it is not their wish or interest to set up for independence; they are merely desirous of preserving their rights.

Before the second Congress assembled, the old jealousy was revived. Adams records how the Sons of Liberty of Philadelphia met the Massachusetts delegates on the road, and warned them to be moderate and "to recognize the lead of Virginia." The "fine fellows" from Virginia, who were "very high," and beside whom the Bostonians were "mere milk-sops," had evidently made an impression. Deane, who was not very apt to be easily impressed, wrote that he had "never met, nor scarcely had an idea of meeting," with such men as the Southern provinces had sent to the Congress. In wealth and social position there could be no contrast, as the Southerners were the "capital men" of the colonies, while, with few exceptions, those from the East were men of "desperate circumstances," risking nothing but their necks in the contest. It was to Virginia that the Presidency of the Congress was given in 1774 and 1775, and when Peyton Randolph left the body, it was on Hancock, the propertied man of the East, that the honor was bestowed. The intimacy between the Adamses and Richard Henry Lee, radicals all, even for that day, in a measure accounts for this division of the honors, and appears to have been the controlling motive for this and subsequent political "deals."

The Massachusetts delegates brought with them the idea of a continental effort, and as early as June 2 the Massachusetts

Massachusetts Congress hinted to the General Congress that as the army then collecting from different colonies was for the general defence of the rights of America, the regulation and control of it was a proper subject for continental action. On the next day Artemas Ward was "from expediency" appointed commander-in-chief by the Provincial Congress, but without any idea of forestalling any action that might be taken at Philadelphia. Learning of this appointment, the New York Congress thought proper to consider a a like appointment in that colony, as "the supposition that in case a continental army should be established, these officers will be permitted to preserve their respective ranks, appears to us highly probable." In Philadelphia the notion of a continental army continually acquired force, until at length action was precipitated, and the step taken—a natural result from the course of events. The question of command now came up for decision.

Early in May, James Warren had expressed the wish that Washington or Lee were in command before Boston—a wish that had probably been inspired by the reports of Washington that the delegates had brought back from the Congress of 1774. Ward was too old to make an efficient commander, and the army too heterogeneous and independent to be easily kept in control. Gates and Lee had reputation for great military knowledge and experience, and Lee especially was much affected by the Eastern delegates. But they were both foreign-born, and both had served in the British establishment, and this was regarded as an objection

objection that overruled what military features were in their favor. Remembering, perhaps, the warning of the Sons of Liberty, and a letter from Warren that may have reached him just before the nomination of Washington would remind him of it—"I should heartily rejoice to see this way the beloved Colonel Washington, and do not doubt the New England generals would acquiesce in *showing to our sister colony, Virginia, the respect*, etc."—Adams suggested Washington, but opposition was made. Many of the delegates thought that as the army was nearly all from New England, had a general of its own, and appeared satisfied with him, Ward should receive the appointment. Fear was expressed that the supersession of the New England generals would lead to discontents and break up the army, as the troops were represented as being bound to their own officers. Adams was positive in the matter, and so was Richard Henry Lee, connected by marriage with Washington; but it rerequired several days of effort to remove the opposition, and when the nomination was at length formally proposed by Washington's friend, Thomas Johnson of Maryland, the choice was made "unanimously." As a compensation, and to equalize the terms of the "deal," the first and third major-generals were taken from the Eastern colonies—Ward and Putnam—and of the eight brigadier-generals, all but one were taken from New England. Respect, surely, had been shown to Virginia, but New England did not suffer her claims to be forgotten; and between the two sections all the officers were divided.

The

The statement of Bancroft that there was only one general officer "who drew to himself the trust and love of his country," is one of those afterthoughts which subsequent events seem to justify. While we find the suggestion of Washington both among the Southern and the Eastern delegates, there was no "general demand" for his election. Indeed, Adams very distinctly states that it was the idea of many "of the staunchest members" of the Congress, and it was the yeast of the activity of a little junto in that body, the Adamses and Lee being its representatives, that leavened the mass. I do not lay much stress on the incident referred to by John Adams, of Washington attending the sessions of Congress in military uniform, thus, as has been suggested, nominating himself for the place. In a few doggerel lines on the Congress of 1774, Drowne says:

> "With manly gait,
> His faithful steel suspended by his side,
> Passed W'-sh-gt-n along, Virginia's hero."

This may be poetic license, but it is quite as probably a statement of fact. Washington may have worn a sword, the House of Burgesses may have worn a uniform when in session, and it may have been this that Adams had in mind. The incident is more curious than important.

No one admitted more frankly the political nature of his election than Washington himself. "The partiality of Congress, joined to a political motive, really left me without a choice," he wrote to his brother, and he

uses

uses nearly the same words in letters to Col. Bassett and the Virginia Military companies. To his wife he wrote as if he had expected the appointment, and could not decline it if it were made :

"You might, and I suppose did perceive, from the tenor of my letters, that I was apprehensive I could not avoid this appointment, as I did not pretend to intimate when I should return. This was the case. It was utterly out of my power to refuse this appointment, without exposing my character to such censures as would have reflected dishonor upon myself and given pain to my friends."

Adams was naturally jubilant over the success of his policy. "This appointment will have a great effect in cementing and securing the union of these colonies." An anonymous writer from Philadelphia said that "Washington, a delegate from Virginia, is, at the particular request of the people of New England," appointed; but this is claiming too much, as the "people" were not so much as consulted, and it is doubtful if the people would have ratified the choice, had it been submitted to them. Gage, with a true insight in the matter, wrote to Dartmouth of "much division in Congress, jealousy of the Eastern delegates, owing to which Washington was appointed to the chief command of the rebel army." The act was, in fact, due to the efforts of a few of the more far-sighted leaders of the Revolution, and was made successful by colonial pride and jealousy.

WORTHINGTON C. FORD.

PARTICULARS OF THE LIFE AND CHARACTER OF GENERAL WASHINGTON.

Extract from a Letter in Lloyd's Evening Post of August 17, [1778] signed an Old Soldier.

Mr. George Washington was the second son of a planter in Virginia, whose situation and circumstances in life were such as might have ranked him with that respectable class of men called the yeomanry. His mother is still living, and so are three brothers and one sister, all married and decently settled in their native colony as planters. By the death of his elder brother Mr. Lawrence Washington, who was a captain in the American troops raised for the expedition against Carthagena, and afterwards incorporated with the regulars, he succeeded to the paternal estate. A late celebrated patriot said in Parliament, that Mr. Washington was an independent gentleman of 5000 l. per annum, clear estate. Many such things are said. It is not usual, however, in that country to estimate men's fortunes by their annual incomes; in fact, owing to many circumstances not necessary here to recite, it is hardly possible this should be done with any precision. His estate, even under his excellent management, never was, one year with another, worth 500 l.

500l. per annum. There are an hundred men in Virginia who have better estates than Mr. Washington; nay five hundred. At his first setting out in life, and before the death of his brother, he was surveyor of the county of Orange; an appointment attended with a good deal of duty, and but little profit. I should imagine it might then (for then it was almost a frontier country, and of course there was more surveying to do) bring him in three or four score pounds a year. Having been used to the woods, and being a youth of great sobriety, diligence, and fidelity, on the first encroachments of the French previous to the last war, he was appointed, by the Assembly of Virginia, to go out to enquire into, and make a report of, the true state of the complaints. He published his Journal, which did credit to his character for care and industry. His appointment soon after to the command of one of the Provincial regiments, and his very decent conduct in that campaign, are facts of sufficient notoriety. One circumstance, perhaps not so generally known, may be mentioned. The very first engagement in which he was ever concerned, was against his own countrymen. He unexpectedly fell in, in the woods, with a party of the other Virginia regiment in the night, and fifty men were killed before the mistake was found out The blame was laid (and possibly with great justness) on the darkness of the night. It is remarkable, however, that the same misfortune befel him in his last action at Germantown; the blame was then also laid on a darkness occasioned by a thick fog.

Before the war was over Mr. Washington resigned, urged

urged thereto by his lady, a widow of Mr. Custis, whom he then married, and which certainly was an advantageous match.

It is not to be denied, that he was not then much liked in the army; but it is not less true that no very good reasons were ever given for his being disliked. I attributed it, (and I hope I may be allowed to have some pretensions to judge of it, having served with him in that campaign,) to his being a tolerably strict disciplinarian; a system which ill suited with the impatient spirits of his headstrong countrymen, who are but little used to restraint. Method and exactness are the *fort* of his character; he gave a very strong proof of this in this very service.

He is not a generous, but a just man; and having, from some idea of propriety, made it a point neither to gain nor lose as an individual in the war, he kept to his purpose, and left the service without either owing a shilling, or being a shilling richer for it.

After his resignation he lived entirely as a country gentleman, distinguished chiefly by his skill and industry in improvements in agriculture. He was a member of the House of Burgesses; respectable, but not shining.

At the time of the stamp act, and during the commencement of the present troubles, he took such a part only as most of his compeers did; save only that being more industrious, and probably less violent, than most of them, he carried the scheme of manufacturing to a greater height than almost any other man.

When it was determined by some restless men in the northern

northern colonies to raise an army, they soon foresaw that it would be impossible to effect this without the concurrence of their southern fellow-colonies; they fixed their eyes, in particular, on Virginia, which having long been called her Majesty's ancient dominion, the people, naturally ostentatious, were proud to be considered as taking the lead. They were artfully indulged and humored in this pardonable instance of human vanity. Mr. Randolph, a Virginian, was made President of the Congress, and Mr. Washington, commander in chief; both of them very honest and well-meaning men. Their honesty betrayed them; for it is an undoubted fact, that they would never have accepted of those posts, if they had not entertained the first and strongest suspicions of their unwarrantable views of their northern brethren. Alas! they considered not how difficult, and even impossible it would be for them, after having once passed the strait line of rectitude, to stop short of the utmost wrong. Their seducers were systematic; and having now prevailed on them, in one great instance, to fly in the face of government, they knew their game too well not to manage so as to cut off all hopes of a retreat. Things were pushed to so desperate an extremity, that safety was now to be found only in going on; the relinquishment of independency, circumstanced as affairs then were, and were contrived to be, would certainly have been to have relinquished also the first ground of the quarrel, the right of taxation.

All this may appear paradoxical, but it is nevertheless

less perfectly consistent with the genuine workings of human nature, and these Americans are not singular in having acted the part I am describing. It is an undoubted fact, that Washington and Randolph (who then acted in concert, and who then also greatly influenced the Colony of Virginia, and, of course, the whole Continent) were, at the time I am speaking of, as adverse to independence, as (for I would express myself strongly) the heads of the northern faction were bent upon it.

But is not his judgment thereby called in question? If independence be now just and advantageous to his country, it must always have been so, and, of course, always his duty to have promoted it.

Placed at the head of an army and country, which, at least, were great and glorious in the American accounts of them, it is not to be wondered at that Mr. Washington soon began to feel his consequence. His ruling passion is military form. Nature has certainly iven him some military talents, yet it is more than probable he never will be a great soldier. There are insuperable impediments in his way. He is but of slow parts, and these are totally unassisted by any kind of education. Now, though such a character may acquit itself with some sort of eclat in the poor, pitiful, unsoldier-like war in which he has hitherto been employed, it is romantic to suppose he must not fail, if ever it should be his lot to be opposed by real military skill. He never saw any actual service but the unfortunate action of Braddock. He never read a book in the art of war of higher value than Bland's exercises;

exercises; and it has already been noted that he is by no means of bright or shining parts. If, then, military knowledge be unlike all other; or, if it be not totally useless as to all the purposes of actual war, it is impossible that Mr. Washington should be a great soldier. In fact, by the mere dint and bravery of our army alone, he has been beaten whenever he has engaged; and that this is left to befal him again, is a problem which, I believe, most military men are utterly at a loss to solve.

It should not be denied, however, that, all things considered, he really has performed wonders. That he is alive to command an army, or that an army is left him to command, might be sufficient to ensure him the reputation of a great General, if the British Generals any longer were what British Generals used to be. In short, I am of the opinion of the Marquis de la Fayette, that any other General in the world than General Howe, would have beaten General Washington; and any other General in the world than General Washington, would have beaten General Howe. I am, &c.,

AN OLD SOLDIER.*

---

* From the *Gentleman's Magazine*, 1778, 368.

CHARACTER OF WASHINGTON.

BY THE REVEREND BENNET ALLEN.

[*From the (London) Morning Post, Tuesday, June 1, 1779.*]

Is a native of Virginia: his first employment was as clerk in Lord Fairfax's land-office, who afterwards made him a land-surveyor, in which capacity he took up most of the best vacant land in the northern neck of Virginia for himself and his brother. By these and other means he possessed himself of a considerable landed property, and became of consequence enough to obtain a command of the Provincial forces in the last war; at the beginning of which he was defeated at a place known by the name of the Little Meadow. He was likewise in Braddock's defeat, and is said to have been useful in bringing off the remains of that corps. This was all the military experience he had an opportunity of gaining. His abilities are of that mediocrity which creates no jealousy; his natural temper makes him reserved, his want of education renders him diffident, and to these negative qualities he seems to have been as much indebted for his appointment and the continuance of his command, as to political motives. The New England delegates concurred in making him the offer of the chief command, to secure the fidelity of Virginia, and the southern provinces; and he pretended that political reasons induced him to accept of it, to preserve a balance of power against the northern provinces. He is ambitious, with the fairest professions of moderation, and avaritious under the most specious appearance of disinterestedness—particularly eager in engrossing large tracts of land, though he has no family, but by a widow lady of fortune he married, who bore children by a former husband. He had not perhaps less than two hundred thousand acres surveyed for him on the Ohio, first purchasing officers' rights for a trifle, and then procuring an order of the council of Virginia to extend the proclamation of 1763 to the Provincials employed in the last war.* It has been a matter of surprize,

---

* *The following extract of a letter from Colonel George Washington to his agent, dated December 27, 1773, will explain a transaction but little known in England :*

"*I have just obtained an order of council to grant lands under the King's proclamation of October, 1763, to the officers and soldiers, by which a lieutenant is entitled to 2000 acres, but that the Governor would not grant his warrants of survey to any that did not personally apply for them. Numbers, however, are obtaining these warrants, and locating them with the surveyors of Augusta, Botetourt, and Fincastle, by whom and their deputies, all these surveys are to be made.*

"*Till I see your brother I am at a loss to locate my own lands under the proclamation of 1763, and am sensible that every day's delay may prove hurtful, as I suppose every officer and soldier within the three provinces, either is or will be upon the move to locate their lands, by which means all the valuable spots will be engrossed.*

G. W."

"*P. S. No land will be granted to any but officers and soldiers.*"

It is evident Washington egregiously outwitted the Governor of Virginia; his request was singularly modest, to include the Provincial officers and soldiers in the grant, for whom the King's proclamation could not design those lands, for this obvious reason, that the object of the war was answered by securing them in possession of their own lands—and to exclude the British officers and

that

that he could so long have made head against the king's forces; but the circumstances of the country all favor the want of skill in the General, and of discipline in the troops.

---

soldiers, for whose reward they were assigned, and to whose distressed families they might hereafter have proved a seasonable refuge, by insisting upon their personal application in Virginia. Many friends of government likewise on the spot were excluded by the grants being only made to the military—and the possession of those lands, as it will afford a safe asylum to the American leaders, if unsuccessful, so it will enlarge their territory to a boundless extent, if they establish independency.

THE AURORA'S FAREWELL TO WASHINGTON.

This virulence of party feeling may be illustrated by the article printed in the *Aurora* of March 6, 1797—the very day on which Jefferson was sworn in as Vice President and on which the retiring President was feted:

FROM A CORRESPONDENT.

"Lord, now lettest thou thy servant depart in peace, for mine eyes have seen thy salvation," was the pious ejaculation of a man who beheld a flood of happiness rushing in upon mankind. If ever there was a time that would license the reiteration of the exclamation, that time is now arrived; for the man who is the source of all the misfortunes of our country, is this day reduced to a level with his fellow citizens, and is no longer possessed of power to multiply evils upon the United States. If ever there was a period for rejoicing, this is the moment—every heart, in unison with the freedom and happiness of the people, ought to beat high with exultation that the name of WASHINGTON from this day ceases to give a currency to political iniquity, and to legalize corruption. A new æra is now opening upon us, an æra which promises much

much to the people; for public measures must now stand upon their own merits, and nefarious projects can no longer be supported by a name. When a retrospect is taken of the WASHINGTONIAN administration for eight years, it is a subject of the greatest astonishment, that a single individual should have cankered the principles of republicanism in an enlightened people, just emerged from the gulph of despotism, and should have carried his designs against the public liberty so far, as to have put in jeopardy its very existence. Such however are the facts, and with these staring us in the face, this day ought to be a JUBILEE in the United States.*

March 4.

---

*This article may with little doubt be attributed to Bache.

In *The Nation* of 28 November, 1889, I wrote of the newspaper attacks on Washington in 1796–97: "The press teemed with attacks upon him and his policy, so bitterly personal in tone and vituperative in language as to excite indignation when read at this late day. None, however, wielded such a bitter pen as a little clique of 'French Democrats' in Philadelphia. Duane, an Irish-American, and Bache, a connection of Benjamin Franklin, formed a partnership, and their paper, the *Aurora*, has never been surpassed, if equalled, in its libellous spirit and neglect of all proprieties. Mr. Henry Adams, in his admirable history, asserts that this paper 'was the nearest approach to a modern newspaper to be found in the country,' and sets him down as a 'scurrilous libeller.' . . . Not content with his [Washington's] retirement, they [the libellers] pursued him into private life, and the farewell to Washington on his leaving the Presidency, penned by Duane, has become a classic of unseemly libel."

In attributing this farewell to the pen of Duane, I followed what had become almost an accepted fact, as the charge had been made again and again in federalist prints during Duane's life, and to my knowledge never denied. But I afterwards found a letter from Duane to the Rev. Mr. Bentley of Salem, Mass., in which he denied the authorship and gives a very interesting account of the cause of Bache's opposition to Washington. I quote the paragraphs pertinent to that matter:—

"Allusion is made in a late *Repertory* to a publication in the *Aurora* of 6

March, 1797, relating to the resignation of Genl. Washington. On the subject of that article my opinion now is of no importance, but as the use of it shows that the cunning and falsehood of Dr. Park are alike adverse to the end which he proposes to obtain, I think it proper to inform you that I was not concerned with the *Aurora* at the time of that publication. Mr. Bache (Dr. Franklin's grandson) was then the editor of the *Aurora*, and I was at that time the editor of the paper now published by Bradford. Mr. Bache died of the yellow fever in September, 1798, and I became editor on the first of November following. So that Dr. Park has either wilfully passed the bounds of veracity or servilely adopted the imposture offence of his coadjutor. I noticed this imposture before in a Connecticut paper, published by a clergyman who formerly edited the *Balance*. I forget his name, but he introduced a letter of Genl. Washington's to Mr. Humphreys, in which allusion is made to Bache's paper; yet this Mr.—aye Mr. Lampper has thought it fit to transfer all the acts of Mr. Bache upon Duane's head. By-the by, I have no objection to accepting all the censure that my predecessor was liable; but it is fit that it should not be done in this disingenuous way.

"Let me have the merit of what I do; and when the question is put to me as to the acts of my predecessor, let me have the manly privilege of showing why and how I undertake to become responsible for them.

"You may not, perhaps, know that the family of Dr. Franklin, and the Doctor himself during his latter years, had not been treated by Genl. Washington as he and they appear to have merited. Indeed, after the Doctor's death his family was in a virtual state of proscription even in the midst of this city, and this state of things too palpably countenanced by the General himself; from what cause it may be in vain to premise, but such was the unpleasant fact; and Mr. Bache, who was in a manner the favorite of Dr. Franklin, was one of those who felt proscription in his family, his industry, and his fortune. It was marked and pointed against him to a degree that you could not conceive without some intimacy with the affairs of the day, and on the spot. Mr. Bache, who next to idolized his grandfather, felt all the culpability that belongs to virtuous minds, and all the indignation of a generous spirit; and he had a right to exult when Genl. Washington felt in his turn the 'slings and arrows of fortune.' He certainly did exult, and with good cause."

INDEX.

Adams, John, 87, 94, 142, 146.
    Samuel, 118.
Addison's Cato, 61 *note*.
Allen, Bennet, 154.
Alton, John, 8.
American Museum, 13.
Appointments in army, 77.
Army, Continental, 48, 49. 144.
          jealousy of, 49, 116.
          character of, 55, 82, 89.
Attack on British proposed, 85, 87.
Aurora on Washington, 157.

Bache, Benjamin Franklin, 158 *note*.
Bancroft, George, 146.
Bassett, Burwell, 147.
Bew, J., 5, 10.
Bibliography, 38.
Billy, 6, 8, 25, 26.
Bishop, John, 8.
Boston, proposed attack on, 51, 53 *note*.
Boucher, Jonathan, 140.
Braddock, 8, 61, 140.
Breechy, 74 *note*.
Bridgey, 74.
Bunker's Hill, 83.

Calvert, Benedict, 59, 67.

Carey, John, 16, 123.
    Mathew, 13.
Carter, Landon, 15, 16 *note*, 112.
Cato, Addison's, 61 *note*.
Civil departments and army, 50.
Colonies, wants of, 48.
Commissioners, English, 75, 93, 99, 105.
Congress, answers and instructions, 83, 87.
    dictates to Washington, 53, *note*.
    interference, 93.
    secrets, 96.
Constitution of Virginia, 112.
Continental Congress, first, 141.
Convention, Virginia, 113.
Conway, Moncure D., 34, 45.
    Thomas, 16, *note*.
Councillors of Virginia, 115.
Critical Review on letters, 10.
Custis, John Parke, 11, 59 *note*.
    children of, 70 *note*.
    Nellie, 67, 70 *note*.
Cutter, C. A., 127, *note*.

Daily Advertiser on letters, 17, 20.
Dandridge, Bat, 116.
Deane, Silas, 143.
Declaration of Independence, 81, 94 *note*, 96, 100.
Delancey, Brigadier General, 6.
Drowne, 146.
Duane, William, 158 *note*.
Duché, Jacob, 13, 130.
Dunmore, Lord, 71, 73 *note*.
Du Simitiere, 32.

Fairfax, Bryan, 142.
"Federal Press," 21.
Fireside generals, 84.

Fleet, British, 84, 94.
Forbes, General, 140.
Ford, Paul Leicester, 12 *note*.
Fortifications, 80, 82.
Fort Lee, 6, 7, 26.
Fort Necessity, 140.
Franklin, Benjamin, 158 *note*.

Gage, General, 142, 147.
Gates, General, 16 *note*, 144.
Germaine, Lord George, 34.
Gordon, William, 26.
Great Britain, reconciliation with, 65, 75, 101.

Hancock, John, 143.
Henry, Patrick, 113, 115.
Hickey plot, 74.
Hildeburne, C. R., 10, 13.
Howe, 69, 99, 102, 109.
Humphreys, James, Jr., 12.

Independency, 48, 65.
Inoculation, 32, 71 *note*.

Jay's treaty, 19.
Jefferson, Thomas, 34, 35, 125.
Joe, 74.
Johnson, Thomas, 145.

Laurens, John, 79.
Lee, Charles, 119, 144.
    Mary, 8.
    Richard Henry, 11, 14, 15, 115
    William (Billy), 8.
Lees of Virginia, 144.
Lexington, 83.
Letter of Howe refused, 102.

Letters, Spurious, editor's preface, 6.
     in loyalist papers, 11.
     notices of, 9, 10.
     objects, 5.
     reprint in 1795, 21.
     Rivington's edition, 12.
     Washington on, 11, 13, 15, 24, 26.
Lynch, Thomas, 53 *note*.

Manual exercise, 63.
McFingal, 30.
Mercer, Hugh, 86, 119.
Mifflin, General, 16 *note*, 73.
Ministry, designs against America, 47, 139.
Monthly Review on letters, 9, 29.

New England, 50, 117.
New York, burning of, 54 *note*.

Officer, character of an, 64.
Official Letters of Washington, 16.

Page, ——, 115.
Paine, Thomas, 119.
Parke, John, 13.
Patterson. Col., 104, 106, 107.
Pickering, Timothy, 26.
Pigott forgeries, 36.
Plot of Hickey, 74.
Putnam, General Israel, 118, 145.

Randolph, Edmund, 33, 140.
    John, 32, 73 *note*.
    Peyton, 143, 151.
Reconciliation with Great Britain, 65, 75, 101.
Republic, want of executive capacity, 88.
Rivington, James, 11, 18, 24.

Robertson, James, 12.
Rumors, 95.

Situation of affairs unknown, 55, 56 *note*.
Small-pox, see Inoculation.
South and North, jealousies of, 117, 142.
Stevens, Henry, 29.
Success a soldier's merit, 61.

Taxation of Colonies, 49, 110.
Tilghman, Tench, 32.
Tories, persecution of, 66.
Town and Country Magazine on letters, 10.
Treaty, Jay, 19.
Trumbull, John, 12, 30.

Vardill, John, 30.
Virginia convention, 113.
    council, 115.
    influence in first Congress, 143.
    new constitution, 112.
    officers troublesome, 78.
    politics, 35.
Virtue, want of public, 48, 53, 56 *note*.

Walker, Benjamin, 24.
War aims only at peace, 75, 86.
    in theory, 63.
    not to be judged by an outsider, 57, 61.
Ward, Artemas, 144, 145.
Warren, James, 144.
Washington, George, abuse of, 19.
    advises Custis, 59
    appointed to be disgraced, 49.
    as a general, 152.
    conduct towards Benj. Franklin, 158 *note*.
    English sympathies, 20.

Washington, George, fears infamy, and disgrace, 46, 57, 80,
    feels a very coward, 46.
    influence of, 141.
    journal, 149.
    land speculations, 155.
    love of country, 46.
    military experience, 140, 152.
    mistrustful, 49.
    mortifications, 87, 87 *note*.
    on appointments, 77.
        independency, 65.
        letters, 11, 13, 15, 24, 26.
        name Rebel, 76.
        reconciliation, 65, 75, 100.
        the military art, 60.
    opinions on, 140, 148.
    policy of, 90 *note*.
    profits of, plantation, 148.
    proposes attack on enemy, 50, 85, 87.
    reasons for accepting command, 48, 138,
        146, 151.
        opposing British, 47, 142.
    refuses Howe's letter, 102.
    reprobates persecution of Tories, 66.
    resignation considered, 56.
    sends papers to Philadelphia, 9.
    sketches of his life, 148, 154.
    will, 8.
    writes to Congress, 93.
Washington, Lawrence, 148.
    Lund, 45 *note*, 73.
    Martha, 69, 95.
        inoculation, 71, 96.
        removal from Mt. Vernon, 72.
        73 *note*.

www.ingramcontent.com/pod-product-compliance
Lightning Source LLC
Chambersburg PA
CBHW031455160426
43195CB00010BB/989